R. E. Hudson

Quartette

containing Songs for the ransomed, Songs of love peace and joy, Gems of gospel song, Salvation echoes

R. E. Hudson

Quartette

containing Songs for the ransomed, Songs of love peace and joy, Gems of gospel song, Salvation echoes

ISBN/EAN: 9783337223007

Printed in Europe, USA, Canada, Australia, Japan

Cover: Foto ©Thomas Meinert / pixelio.de

More available books at **www.hansebooks.com**

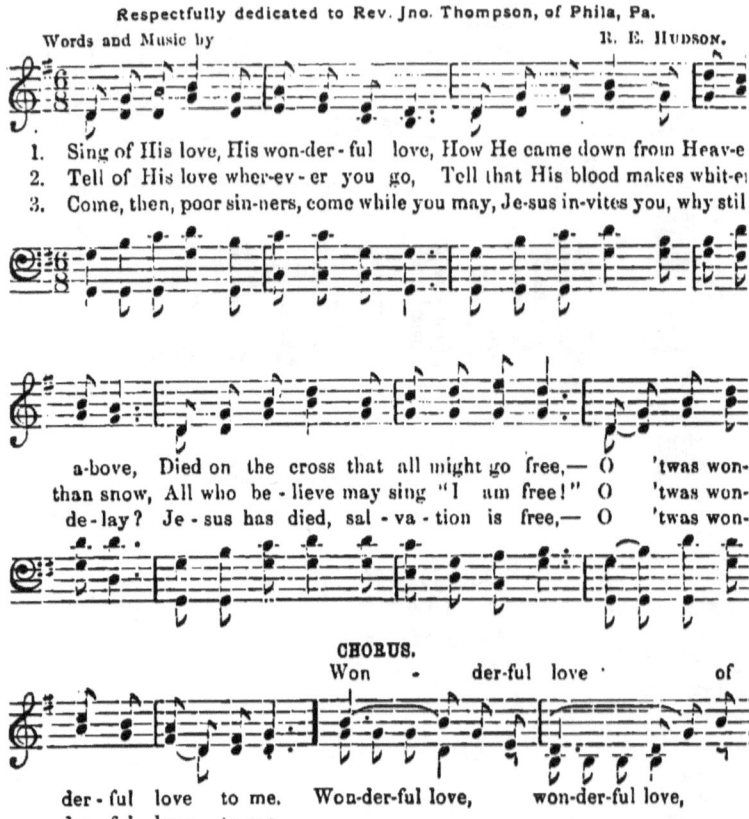

4. WHEN THE GLAD DAY COMES.

Words and Music by SILVER LAKE QUARTETTE, by per.

1. We will shout our loud ho-san-nas When the glad day comes, We will proud-ly wave our ban-ners When the glad day comes: For the wide world will be bet-ter, All man-kind will be our debt-or, If on rum, we forge a fet-ter, When the glad day comes. And it comes;
2. Then be read-y for the bat-tle, Till the glad day comes; Nev-er fear the roar and rat-tle When the glad day comes: Tho' our foe be so ap-pall-ing, And a-round us men are fall-ing, Hear the Right's clear bu-gle call-ing, Till the glad day comes.
3. Men of God, the time is near-ing, When the glad day comes: Look a-loft! the skies are clear-ing, For the glad day comes: With the world of truth, your tok-en, Keep your cour-age all un-brok-en, For be-hold! the Lord hath spok-en, And the glad day comes.

CHORUS.

Yes, it comes;

WHEN THE GLAD DAY COMES.—Concluded.

comes; Soon we'll hear the music ringing, From the glad hearts
Yes, it comes;
it is bringing, And the world will join in singing, When the glad day comes.

PRESS THIS BATTLE ON. 5.
R. E. HUDSON.

1. Sold-iers of Christ, a-rise, And put your arm-or on,
Cho.— We'll press this bat-tle on, We'll press this bat-tle on,
2. Strong in the Lord of hosts, And in his might-y pow'r,
3. Stand, then, in His great might, With all His strength en-dued;
4. That, hav-ing all things done, And all your con-flicts passed,

Strong in the strength which God supplies, Thro' His e-ter-nal Son;
In Je-sus' might we'll stand and fight, And press this bat-tle on.
Who in the strength of Je-sus trusts Is more than con-quer-or.
But take, to arm you for the fight, The pan-o-ply of God;
Ye may o'er-come thro' Christ a-lone, And stand en-tire at last.

Copyrighted, 1884, by R. E. HUDSON.

8. FATHER'S HOUSE.

Respectfully dedicated to Rev. S. C. Swallow, Harrisburg, Pa.

R. E. HUDSON.

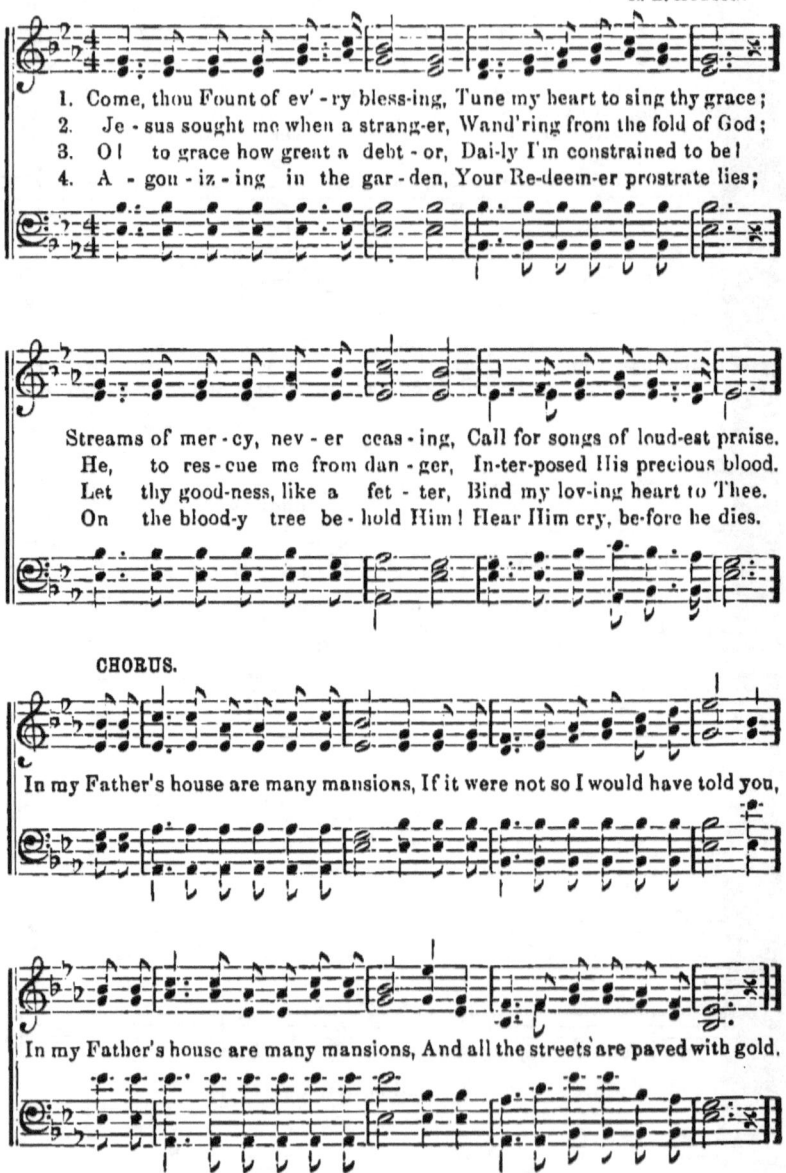

1. Come, thou Fount of ev'-ry bless-ing, Tune my heart to sing thy grace;
2. Je - sus sought me when a strang-er, Wand'ring from the fold of God;
3. O! to grace how great a debt - or, Dai-ly I'm constrained to be!
4. A - gon - iz - ing in the gar - den, Your Re-deem-er prostrate lies;

Streams of mer - cy, nev - er ceas - ing, Call for songs of loud-est praise.
He, to res - cue me from dan - ger, In-ter-posed His precious blood.
Let thy good-ness, like a fet - ter, Bind my lov-ing heart to Thee.
On the blood-y tree be - hold Him! Hear Him cry, be-fore he dies.

CHORUS.

In my Father's house are many mansions, If it were not so I would have told you,

In my Father's house are many mansions, And all the streets are paved with gold.

10. WASH ME IN THE BLOOD.

COWPER.   E. O. EXCELL, by per.

1. There is a foun-tain filled with blood, Drawn from Im-man-uel's veins,
   And sin-ners plunged be-neath that flood, Lose all their guilt-y stains.
2. The dy-ing thief re-joiced to see That foun-tain in his day,
   And there may I, tho' vile as he, Wash all my sins a-way.
3. Thou dy-ing Lamb, thy pre-cious blood Shall nev-er lose its pow'r,
   Till all the ransomed Church of God Are saved, to sin no more.

CHORUS.

Sav-iour, wash . . . me in the blood, . . . Sav-iour, wash . . . me in the blood, . . . Oh, wash . . . me
Sav-iour, wash me in the blood, in the blood of the Lamb, Sav-iour, wash me in the blood, in the blood of the Lamb, Oh, wash me in the blood,

WONDROUS LOVE.—Concluded.

'Twas for me that Je-sus suffered On the Cross of Cal-va-ry.

Copyrighted, 1886, by R. E. Hudson.

HAPPY ON THE WAY. 13.

R. E. HUDSON.

1. { Oh, good old way, how sweet thou art, / May none of us from Thee de-part; } Bless the Lord, I'm
2. { But may our ac-tions al-ways say, / We're marching in the good old way, } Bless the Lord, I'm
3. { This note a-bove the rest shall swell, / That Je-sus do-eth all things well, } Bless the Lord, I'm

1st. 2d. CHORUS.

hap-py on the way, way. Hap-py on the way, Hap-py
hap-py on the way, way.
hap-py on the way, way.

on the way, Bless the Lord, I'm hap py on the way.

Copyrighted, 1886, by R. E. Hudson.

LET ME HIDE IN THY WOUNDS. 19.

Words and Music by E. A. HOFFMAN.

1. O Jesus! when wounded with sin, I flee to the cleft of thy side;
2. When thirsting for fulness of love, And deeper communion with thee,
3. When nearing the shadowy vale, The darkness enshrouding my sight,

I leave all my sorrow and fear, And trust in the "Once Crucified."
I haste to the cleft of thy side, Where blessing is waiting for me.
I'll hide me in peace in thy wounds, Till bathed in yon heavenly light.

CHORUS.

O Lord, in thy wounds let me hide, In the
O Lord, in thy wounds let me

wounds of the Saviour crucified, In the cleft, in the cleft of thy
hide, In the wounds of the Saviour crucified, In the

side, Blessed Saviour of sinners, let me hide, let me hide.
cleft of thy side,

22. DEATH IS COMING.

R. E. HUDSON.

1. Sin-ners, whith-er will you wan-der? Whith-er will you stray?
2. Sa-tan has re-solved to have you For his law-ful prey;
3. Lis-ten to the in-vi-ta-tion, While He's cry-ing, come;
4. Soon you'll see the Lord de-scend-ing On His great white throne,

O re-mem-ber life is slen-der, 'Tis but a short day.
Je-sus Christ has died to save you; Haste, O haste a-way.
If you miss the great sal-va-tion Hell will be your doom.
Saints and sin-ners all at-tend-ing To re-ceive their doom.

CHORUS.

Death is com-ing, com-ing, com-ing, And the judgment day.

Hast-en, sin-ner, hast-en, sin-ner, Seek the nar-row way.

Copyrighted, 1886, by R. E. HUDSON.

I COME JUST AS I AM. 23.

Copyrighted, 1884, by R. E. Hudson.

26. WEARY ONE, REST.

R. E. HUDSON.

1. I heard the voice of Jesus say: "Come unto me and rest!
2. I came to Jesus as I was, Weary, and worn, and sad;
3. I heard the voice of Jesus say: "Behold! I freely give
4. I came to Jesus, and I drank Of that life-giving stream;

CHORUS.

Lay down, poor weary one, Lay down your head upon my breast. Jesus is
I found in Him a resting-place, And He has made me glad.
The living water—thirsty one, Stoop down, and drink, and live."
My thirst was quenched, my soul is saved, And now I live in Him.

waiting, Jesus is waiting, Jesus is waiting for you and me;

Jesus is waiting, Jesus is waiting, Jesus is waiting for thee.

Copyrighted, 1885, by R. E. HUDSON

JESUS IS STRONG TO DELIVER. 27.

Words and Music by H. H. B.

1. When in the tem-pest He'll hide us, When in the storm He'll be near; All the way long He will car-ry us on, Now we have noth-ing to fear.
2. When in my sor-row He found me, Found me and bade me be whole; Turned all my night in-to heav-en-ly light, From me my bur-den did roll.
3. Why are you doubt-ing and fear-ing? Why are you still un-der sin? Have you not found that His grace doth a-bound? Might-y to save; let Him in.
4. You say: "I'm weak, I am help-less, I've tried a-gain and a-gain;" This may be true, but it's not what *you* do, He is the "Might-y to save!"

CHORUS.

Je-sus is strong to de-liv-er! Might-y to save! might-y to save! Je-sus is strong to de-liv-er! Je-sus is might-y to save!

2. At the well of Jacob, resting by its brink,
Bidding the Samaritan give to him to drink,
When she asked of Jesus where men ought to pray,
At the well of Jacob, what did Jesus say?
[JOHN iv : 21, 23.]

3. On the sea of Galilee, when the storm was high,
Save us, Lord! we perish! his disciples cry;
While they marvel greatly, as the winds obey,
On the sea of Galilee, what did Jesus say?
[MATT. viii : 26.]

4. Coming into Bethany, meeting, full of gloom,
Martha, mourning Lazarus, lying in the tomb—
Of the Resurrection, and the last Great Day,
Coming into Bethany, what did Jesus say?
[JOHN xi : 23, 25.]

5. Weeping o'er Jerusalem, city of the King,
Whom he would have gathered 'neath his loving wing,
Mourning for her children, going far astray,
Weeping o'er Jerusalem, what did Jesus say?
[MATT. xxiii : 37.]

6. From that cross of sorrow, ere his soul went up,
As he drank the fullness of the bitter cup,
Looking on his enemies, in their dark array,
From that cross of sorrow, what did Jesus say?
[LUKE xxiii : 34.]

7. On the hills of heaven, in the world above,
Where his faithful children share his wondrous love,
All their sins forgiven, in that blessed day,
On the hills of heaven, what will Jesus say?
[MATT. xxv : 34.]

30. TREASURES OF HEAVEN.

By per. T. C. O'Kane.

1. There's a crown in heaven for the striv-ing soul, Which the bless-ed Je-sus him-self will place On the head of each who shall faith-ful prove Even un-to death in the heavenly race, Oh, may that crown in heaven be mine, And I a-mong the an-gels shine; Be thou, O Lord! my daily guide, Let me ev-er in thy love a-bide.

2. There's a Rest in heaven for the wea-ry soul, 'Tis for all by care and by sin oppressed; To the sons of God it re-main-eth sure, And the Prophet says, 'tis a "glorious rest," Oh, may that Rest in heaven be mine, And I among the angels shine; Be thou, oh Lord! my daily guide, Let me ev-er in thy love a-bide.

3. There's a home in heaven for the faith-ful soul, In the man-y man-sions pre-pared a-bove, Where the glo-ri-fied shall for-ev-er sing, Of a Saviour's free and unbounded love, Oh, may that Home in heaven be

I'M SATISFIED.—Concluded.

love has won my heart, won my heart, And now He sets me free.

Copyrighted, 1886, by R. E. Hudson.

SITTING AT THE FEET OF JESUS. 33.

Priscilla J. Owens.   E. S. Lorenz.

1. O the peace that fills my soul, Sitting at the feet of Jesus;
2. Christ is mine in storm and calm; Sitting at the feet of Jesus;
3. Here I rest from toil and strife, Sitting at the feet of Jesus;

Cleansed from sin, made free and whole, Sitting at the feet of Jesus.
All my wounds are filled with balm, Sitting at the feet of Jesus.
Safe beneath the Tree of Life, Sitting at the feet of Jesus.

CHORUS.

This is my abiding place, Clothed with His abounding grace,

Looking upward to His face, Sitting at the feet of Jesus.

Copyrighted, 1885, by E. S. Lorenz.

THE BURDEN BEARER.—Concluded.

Copyrighted, 1889, by I. N. McHose.

HE CAME TO SAVE ME. 35.

H. E. Blair. Wm. J. Kirkpatrick, by per.

1. { When Jesus laid His crown aside, He came to save me;
     When on the cross He bled and died, ... He came to save me.
2. { In my poor heart He deigns to dwell, He came to save me;
     Oh, praise His name, I know it well, ... He came to save me.

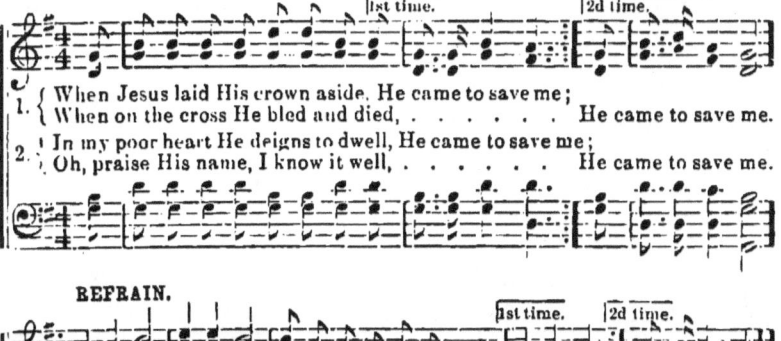

REFRAIN.

I'm so glad, I'm so glad, I'm so glad that Jesus came, And grace is free,
He . . . came to save me.

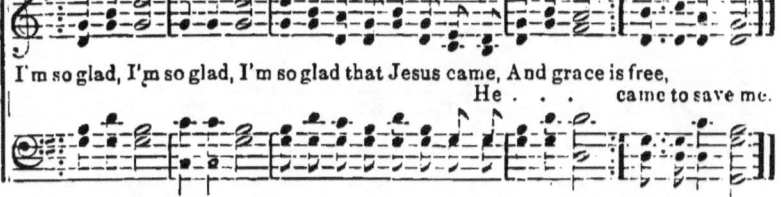

3 With gentle hand He leads me still,
    He came to save me;
  And trusting Him I fear no ill,
    He came to save me.

4 To Him my faith with rapture clings,
    He came to save me;
  To Him my heart looks up and sings,
    He came to save me.

Copyright, 1885, by Wm. J. Kirkpatrick.

THE UNSEEN CITY.—Concluded. 37

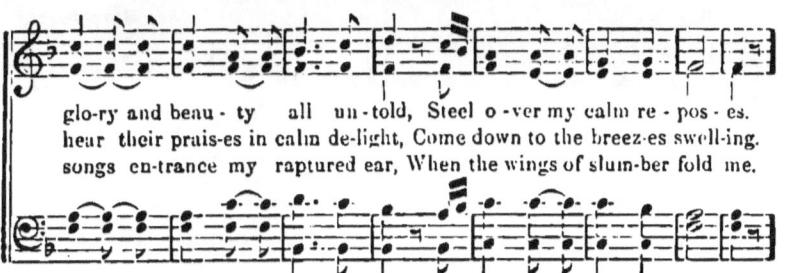

glo-ry and beau-ty all un-told, Steel o-ver my calm re-pos-es.
hear their prais-es in calm de-light, Come down to the breez-es swell-ing.
songs en-trance my raptured ear, When the wings of slum-ber fold me.

CHORUS.

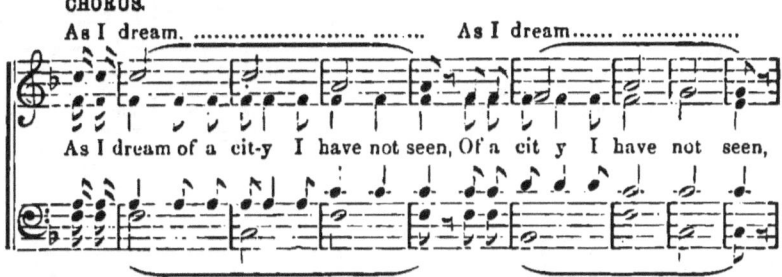

As I dream............... As I dream...............
As I dream of a cit-y I have not seen, Of a cit-y I have not seen,

Of a cit-y I have not seen, As I dream...............
As I dream,............ As I dream of a cit-y I have not seen,

As I dream............... of a cit-y I have not seen.
Of a cit-y I have not seen, Of a cit-y I have not seen.

By permission of S. BRAINALD Y SONS, owners of copyright.

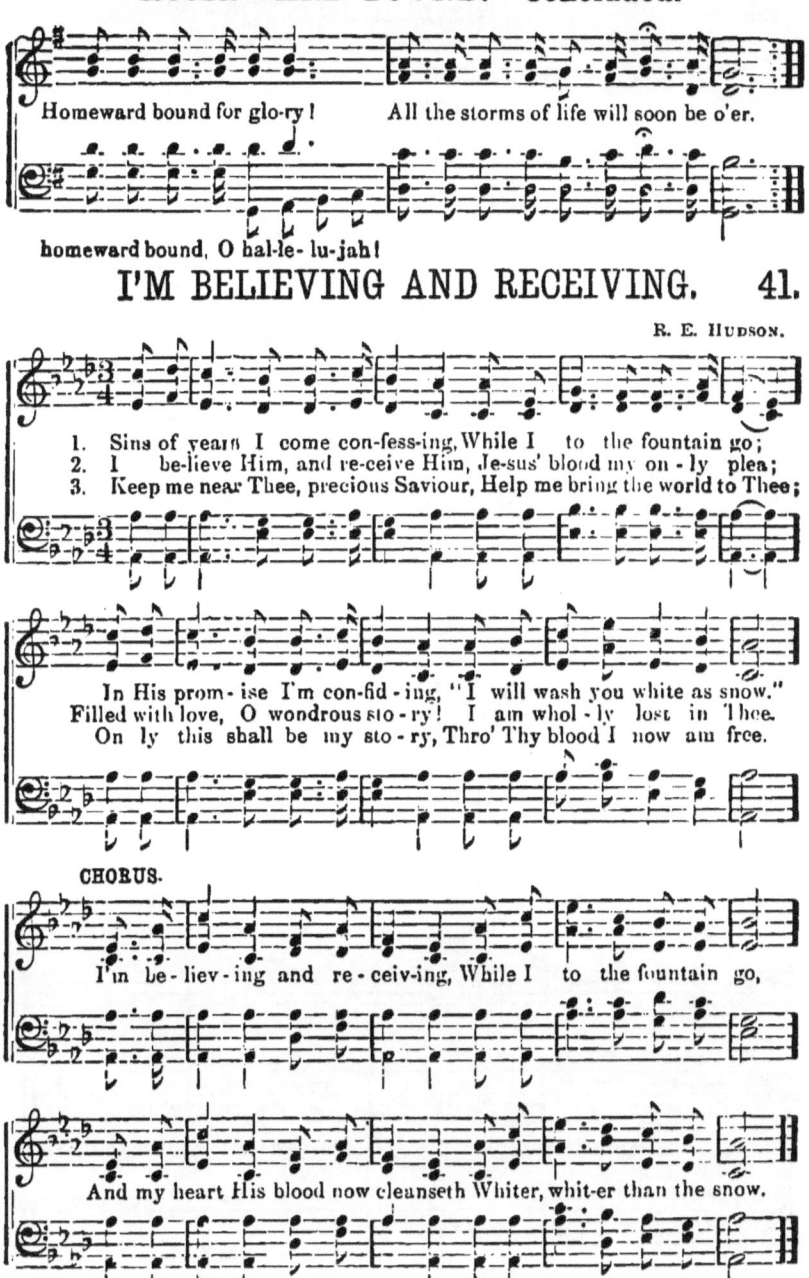

Handwriting on the Wall.—Concluded.

Copyrighted by E. O. Excell.

ROLL THE STONE AWAY. 45.

Dedicated to W. C. T. U. of the United States. R. E. Hudson.

1. Lo! the night of ease is past, Ac-tion comes, in love, at last,
2. It has filled our hap-py land With its wrecks on ev-'ry hand,
3. Ye who pi-ty, ye who feel, Lis-ten now to our ap-peal,
4. Un-to Thee we look for power, Help us in this cri-sis hour,

As we hail the dawning day; Who shall roll the stone a-way?
While the helpless vic-tims pray, Roll this dreadful stone a-way.
All who sym-pathize and pray, Help us roll the stone a-way.
Bring the dawning of the day, Roll, oh, roll the stone a-way.

CHORUS. Roll........ the stone a-way,
Roll the stone, the stone a-way, Brothers, roll, while sis-ters pray,

Join to-geth-er heart and hand, And roll the stone a-way.

MEET ME THERE.—Concluded.

Where the Tree of Life is blooming, Meet me there. When the
Meet me there.

TAKE ALL MY SINS AWAY. 47.

MARECHALE BOOTH. MARECHALE BOOTH.

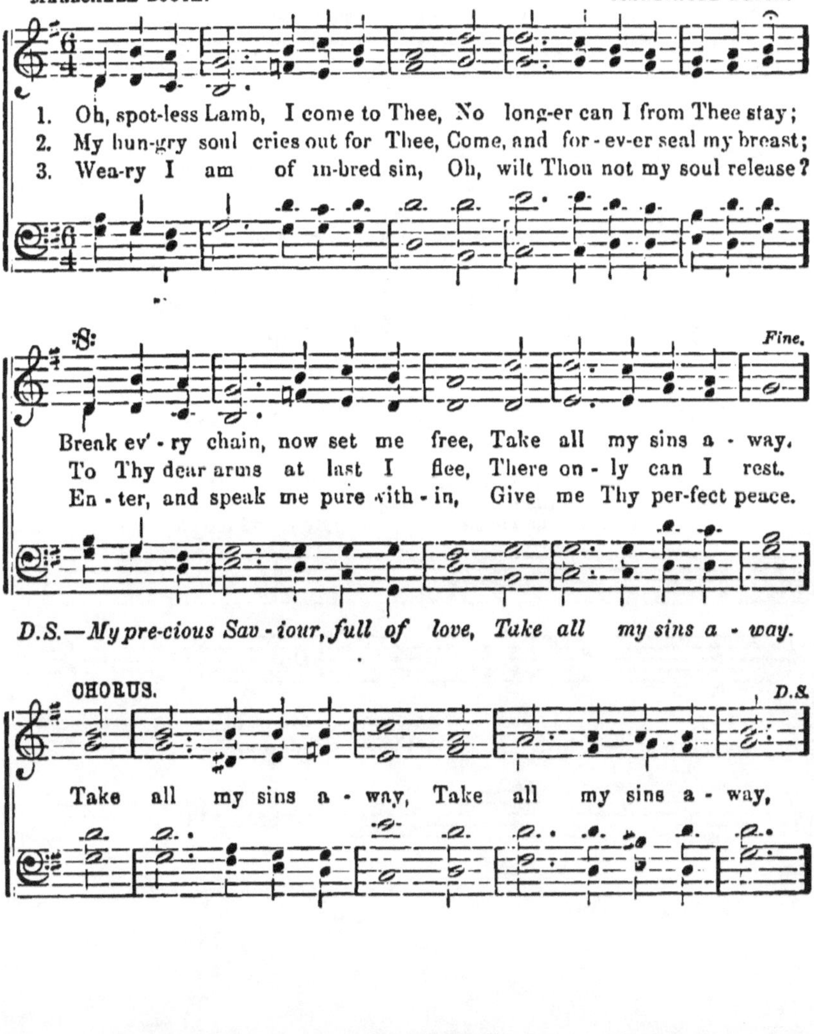

1. Oh, spot-less Lamb, I come to Thee, No long-er can I from Thee stay;
2. My hun-gry soul cries out for Thee, Come, and for-ev-er seal my breast;
3. Wea-ry I am of in-bred sin, Oh, wilt Thou not my soul release?

Break ev'-ry chain, now set me free, Take all my sins a-way.
To Thy dear arms at last I flee, There on-ly can I rest.
En-ter, and speak me pure with-in, Give me Thy per-fect peace.

D.S.—My pre-cious Sav-iour, full of love, Take all my sins a-way.

CHORUS.

Take all my sins a-way, Take all my sins a-way,

He Rolled the Clouds Away.—Concluded.

He hath spok-en, And rolled the clouds, the clouds a-way.

Copyrighted, 1885, by R. E. Hudson.

OLD, YET EVER NEW. 49.

W. A. Williams, by per.

1. There is a sto-ry sweet to hear, I love to tell it, too: It fills my
2. They tell me God the Son came down From His bright throne to die, That I might
3. They say He bore the cross for me, And suffered in my place, That I might
4. O wondrous love! so great, so vast, So boundless and so free! Low at thy

CHORUS.

heart with hope and cheer,'Tis old, yet ever new. 'Tis old, yet ev-er new; 'Tis
wear a starry crown, And dwell with Him on high.
always happy be, And ransomed by His grace.
feet my all I cast; I cov-et on-ly Thee. 'Tis old,

old, yet ev-er new; I know, I feel it's true: 'Tis old, but ever new.
   'Tis old,   I know,

BEAUTIFUL CITY OF GOLD.—Concluded.

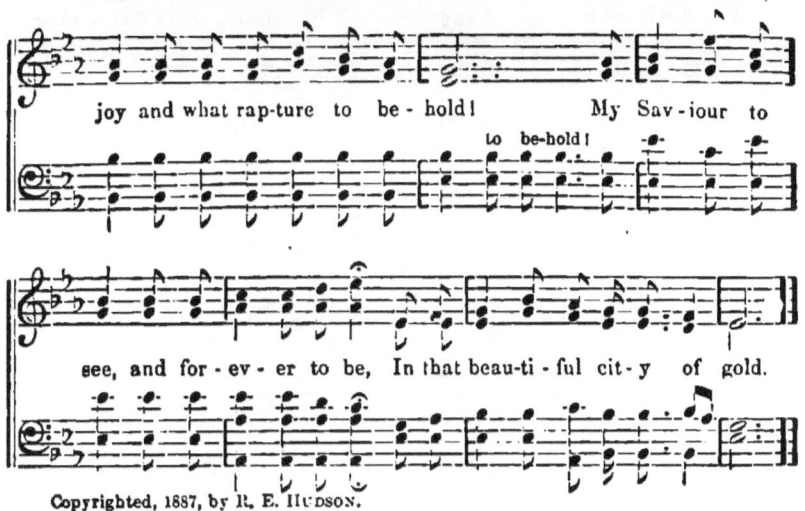

joy and what rap-ture to be-hold! My Sav-iour to see, and for-ev-er to be, In that beau-ti-ful cit-y of gold.

Copyrighted, 1887, by R. E. Hudson.

MEDITATION. 55

JOSEPH SWAIN.   FREEMAN LEWIS.

1. O thou, in whose presence my soul takes delight, On whom in affliction I call,
2. O why should I wander, an alien from Thee, Or cry in the desert for bread?
3. Ye daughters of Zion, declare, have you seen The Star that on Israel shone?
4. Dear Shepherd! I hear, and will follow thy call; I know the sweet sound of thy

[voice;

My comfort by day, and my song in the night, My hope, my salvation, my all!
Thy foes will rejoice when my sorrows they see, And smile at the tears I have shed.
Say, if in your tents my Beloved has been, And where with his flocks he is gone.
Restore and defend me, for Thou art my all, And in Thee I will ever rejoice.

Who's on the Lord's Side?—Concluded.

col-ors—who's on the Lord's side? Oh, who is there a-mong us, the true and the tried, Who'll stand by His col-ors—who's on the Lord's side?

HE IS CALLING. 59.

FABER. Arranged by S. J. VAIL, by per.

1. There's a full-ness in God's mer-cy, Like the full-ness of the sea;
2. There's no place where earth-ly sor-rows Are more felt than up in heav'n;
3. For the love of God is broad-er Than the meas-ure of man's mind:
4. If our love were but more sim-ple, We should take Him at his word;

There's a kind-ness in His jus-tice Which is more than lib-er-ty.
There's no place where earth-ly fail-ings Have such kind-ly judgment giv'n.
And the heart of the E-ter-nal Is most won-der-ful-ly kind.
And our lives would be all sun-shine In the sweet-ness of our Lord.

REFRAIN.
He is call-ing, "Come to me;" Lord, I'll glad-ly haste to thee.

MARCHING ON. 61.

Words and Music by Capt. Johnson.

1. Marching on in the light of God, Marching on, I am marching on;
2. Marching on thro' the hosts of sin, Marching on, I am marching on;
3. Marching on while the skeptics sneer, Marching on, I am marching on;
4. Marching on with the flag un-furled, Marching on, I am marching on;

Up the path that the Mas-ter trod. March-ing, march-ing on.
Vic-t'ry's mine, while I've Christ with-in, March-ing, march-ing on.
Per-fect love cast-eth out all fear, March-ing, march-ing on.
Preach-ing Christ to the dy-ing world, March-ing, march-ing on.

CHORUS.

A robe of white, a crown of gold, A harp, a home, a mansion fair,

A vic-tor's palm, a joy un-told, Are mine when I get there.

Copyrighted, 1887, by R. E. Hudson.

64. MIGHTY MARCH.

I. N. McHose, by per.

1. Conquering God, go forth in gran-deur, Bless-ed Christ, as-sert Thy sway; Ho-ly Spir-it, lift the peo-ple Out of dark-ness in-to day.
2. Pray'r is an-swered; lo! the vic-t'ry! High-est mount and deep-est glen; Roll the bless-ed tid-ing on-ward, Je-sus Christ is sav-ing men.
3. Like the sound of man-y wa-ters From a choir ten thou-sand strong, Swells the ev-er widening glo-ry, Swells sal-va-tion's sweet-est song.

CHORUS.

Spread the an-them high as heav'n, Spread the an-them high as heav'n, Raise the grand tri-umph-al arch, Raise the grand tri-umph-al arch, Make way, con-ti-nents and na-tions,

HIS NAME IS JESUS.—Concluded.

For He saves! For He saves! For He saves His peo-ple from their sins.

Copyrighted, 1886, by R. E. Hudson.

BLESSED NAME. 67.

R. E. Hudson.

1. { O for a thousand tongues to sing: Bless-ed be the name of the Lord!
   { The glo-ries of my God and King, Bless-ed be the name [*Omit*........
2. { Je-sus, the name that charms our fears, Blessed be the name of the Lord!
   { 'Tis mu-sic in the sin-ner's ear, Bless-ed be the name [*Omit*........
3. { He breaks the pow'r of cancelled sin, Bless-ed be the name of the Lord!
   { His blood can make the foul-est clean, Bless-ed be the name [*Omit*........
4. { I nev-er shall for-get that day, Bless-ed be the name of the Lord!
   { When Je-sus washed my sins a-way, Bless-ed be the name [*Omit*........

2d.

CHORUS.

of the Lord!
of the Lord!
of the Lord!
of the Lord!

Bless-ed be the name, Bless-ed be the name,

1st. 2d.

Bless-ed be the name of the Lord! Bless-ed be the name of the Lord!

Copyrighted, 1886, by R. E. Hudson.

68. We Shall Stand Before the King.

Words and Music by E. O. EXCELL.

We Shall Stand Before the King.—Concluded.

...fore the King, With the an-gels we shall sing, Glo-ry
be-fore the King,

glo-ry to our King! Hal-le-lu - jah! hal-le-
Hal - le - lu - jah!

lu - jah! We shall stand ... be-fore the King.
Hal - le - lu - jah! We shall stand

Copyrighted, 1885, by E. O. Excell.

THE ROAD TO HEAVEN. 69.

1. { The road to heav'n by Christ was made, With heav'nly truth the rails are laid, }
   { From earth to heav'n the line ex-tends, To life e-ter-nal where it ends. }

2. { Re-pen-tance is the sta-tion, then, Where pas-sen-gers are tak-en in; }
   { No fee for them is there to pay, For Je-sus is him-self the way. }

3. { The Bi-ble is the en-gi-neer—It points the way to heav'n so clear, }
   { Thro' tun-nels dark and dreary here— It leads to glo-ry, nev-er fear. }

4. { God's love the fire, his truth the way, Which leads us home to endless day; }
   { All you who would to glo-ry ride, Must come to Christ—in him abide. }

5. { Come, then, poor sin-ner, now is the time, At an-y sta-tion on the line; }
   { If you re-pent, and turn from sin, The train will stop, and take you in. }

CHORUS.

We're go-ing home, We're go-ing home, To die no more, To die no more.

I Shall Never Know a Sorrow.—Concluded.

with the glo-ry in my soul, I shall nev-er know a sorrow o-ver there! over there!

Copyrighted, 1885, by E. E. NICKERSON.

ANGELS ARE LOOKING ON ME. 89.

REV. JOHN PARKER.   Arranged.

1. Like Ja-cob, in his Beth-el rest, The an-gels are look-ing on me;
2. Each night I lay me down to sleep, The an-gels are look-ing on me;
3. And when I wake, new toils to meet, The an-gels are look-ing on me;
4. I lay me down at night to sleep, The an-gels are look-ing on me;

They watch my pil-low—I am blest, The an-gels are look-ing on me.
I know I'm safe, for an-gels keep, The an-gels are look-ing on me.
God's presence makes my joy com-plete, The an-gels are look-ing on me.
I pray the Lord my soul to keep, While an-gels are look-ing on me.

REFRAIN.

All night, all night The an-gels are look-ing on me;

All night, all night The an-gels are look-ing on me.

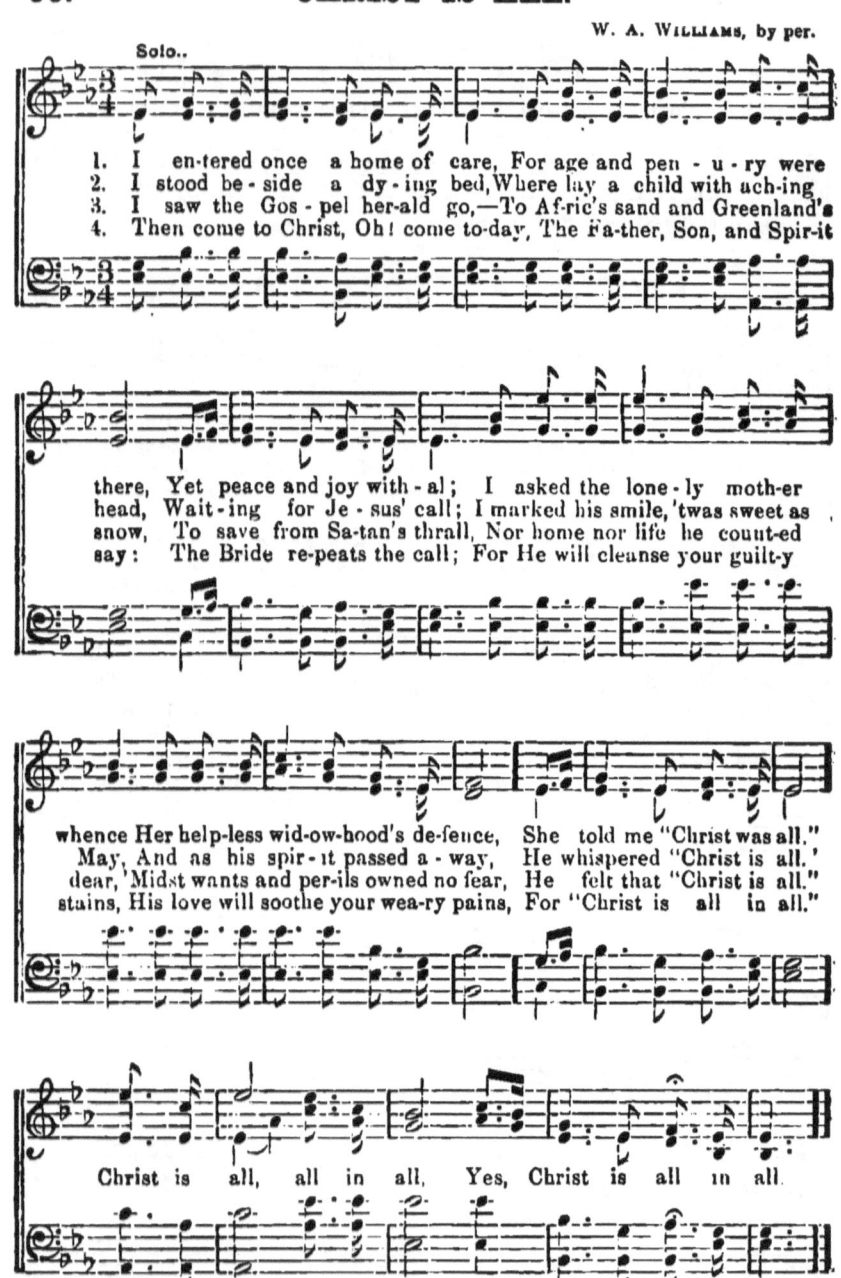

THE TEN VIRGINS. 91.

Words and Music by R. E. HUDSON.

1. Five of them were wise when the Bridegroom came,
2. Five of them were fool-ish when the Bridegroom came,
3. The wise took their oil when the Bridegroom came,
4. The fool-ish had no oil when the Bridegroom came.
5. The right-eous were ac-cept-ed when the Bridegroom came,
6. The fool-ish were re-ject-ed when the Bridegroom came,
7. Will you all be read-y when the Bridegroom comes?

Five of them were wise when the Bride-groom came,
Five of them were fool-ish when the Bride-groom came,
The wise took their oil when the Bride-groom came,
The fool-ish had no oil when the Bride-groom came,
The right-eous were ac-cept-ed when the Bride-groom came,
The fool-ish were re-ject-ed when the Bride-groom came,
Will you all be read-y when the Bride-groom comes?

And trust-ing, oh, trust-ing, yes, trust-ing when the Bridegroom came.
And doubt-ing, oh, doubt-ing, yes, doubt-ing when the Bridegroom came.
And sing-ing, oh, sing-ing, yes, sing-ing when the Bridegroom came.
And weep-ing, oh, weep-ing, yes, weep-ing when the Bridegroom came.
And shout-ing, oh, shout-ing, yes, shout-ing when the Bridegroom came.
And wail-ing, oh, wail-ing, yes, wail-ing when the Bridegroom came.
And wait-ing, oh, wait-ing, yes, wait-ing when the Bridegroom comes.

Copyrighted, 1881, by R. E. HUDSON.

COMING HOME TO-NIGHT.—Concluded.

boy she loves, to her so dear, Is com-ing home to-night.

Copyrighted, 1882, by R. E. Hudson.

ALONE WITH JESUS. 93.
[For Male Voices.]

Mrs. H. B. Beegle. J. H. Tenney.

1. A-lone with Je-sus! oh, how sweet To bow sub-mis-sive at His feet!
2. A-lone with Je-sus! bless-ed rest, While by His constant presence blest,
3. A-lone with Je-sus! let me stay While earth-ly com-forts pass a-way;

To bid my trembling heart be still, And calm-ly sink in-to His will;
With ev'-ry i-dol brok-en down, And in my heart He reigns a-lone;
Till ev'-ry earth-ly prop shall fall, And Christ, my Lord, be all in all;

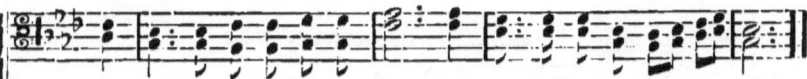

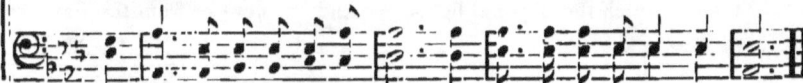

For-get-ting all my cares and woes, And in His lov-ing arms re-pose!
While in my soul His love is shed, And roy-al bless-ings crown my head.
Till in His glo-ry He shall come, And bring His ransomed children home.

Copyrighted, 1881, by R. E. Hudson.

JUST THE SAME TO-DAY.—Concluded.

I'm glad to tell you, sin-ner, He is just the same to-day.

Copyrighted, 1885, by I. N. McHose.

WONDERFUL SAVIOUR. 97.

Words and Music by ELISHA A. HOFFMAN, by per.

1. Christ has for sin a-tone-ment made—What a won-der-ful
2. I praise Him for the cleans-ing blood, What a won-der-ful
3. To Him I've giv-en all my heart, What a won-der-ful

Sav-iour! We are re-deemed! the price is paid! What a
Sav-iour! That rec-on-ciled my soul to God; What a
Sav-iour! The world shall nev-er share a-part; What a

CHORUS.

won-der-ful Sav-iour! What a won-der-ful Sav-iour is Je-sus,
won-der-ful Sav-iour!
won-der-ful Sav-iour!

my Je-sus! What a won-der-ful Sav-iour is Je-sus, my Lord!

100. O TO BE NOTHING!

R. E. HUDSON.

Slow.

D.C.—1. O to be noth-ing, noth-ing, On-ly to lie at His feet; A brok-en and empt-ed ves-sel, For the Mas-ter's use made meet; Emp-tied that He might fill me, As forth to His serv-ice I go, Brok-en, that so un-hin-dered, His life through me might flow.

2. O to be noth-ing, noth-ing, On-ly as led by His hand; A mes-sen-ger at His gate-way, On-ly wait-ing His com-mand; On-ly an a-gent, read-y His prais-es to sound at His will, Will-ing, should He not call me, In si-lence trust Him still.

3. O to be noth-ing, noth-ing, Pain-ful the hum-bling may be, Yet low in the dust I'd lay me, To bring the world to Thee; Rath-er be noth-ing, noth-ing— To Him let their voic-es be raised, He is the fount of bless-ing, His name the world shall praise.—D.C.

Copyrighted, 1887, by R. E. HUDSON.

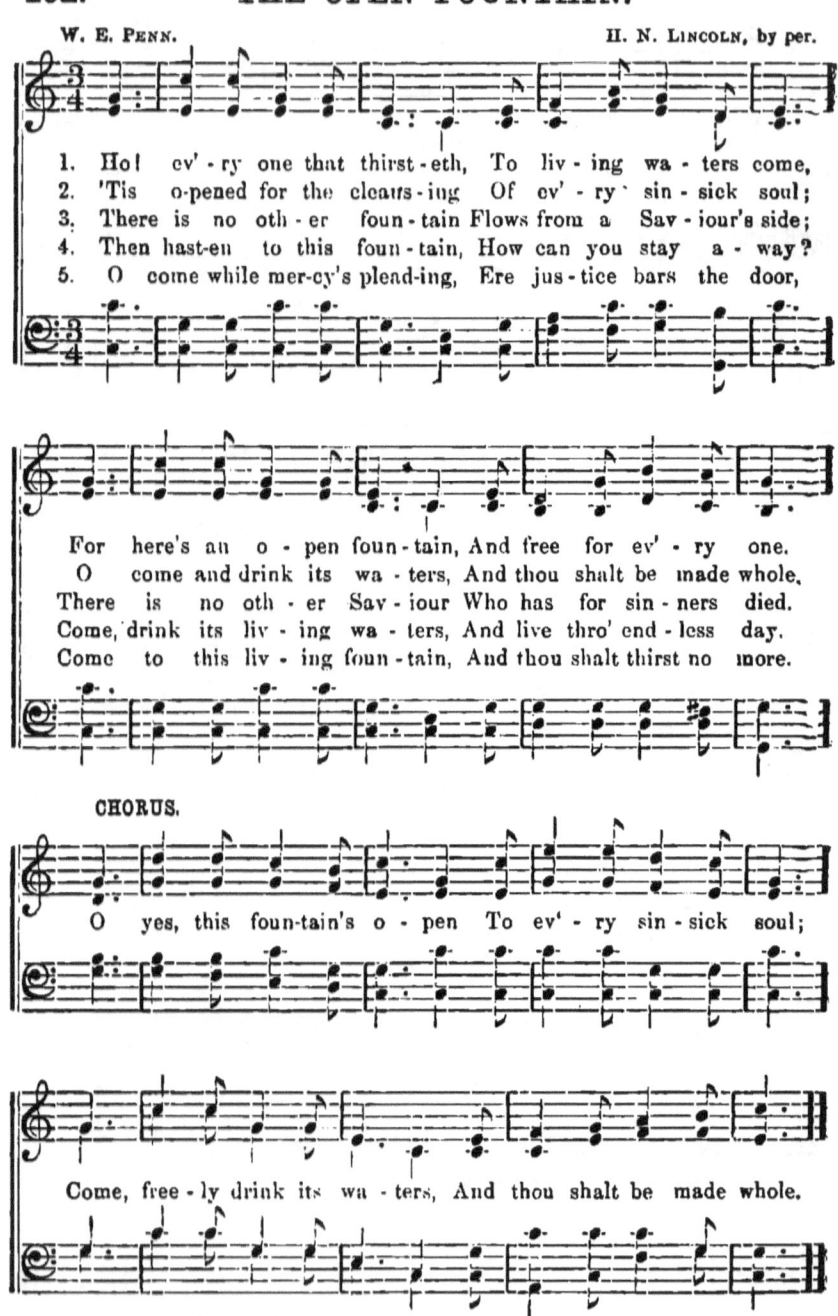

104. SOME SWEET DAY.

ARTHUR W. FRENCH.   D. B. TOWNER, by per.

1. We shall reach the riv-er side, Some sweet day, some sweet day;
2. We shall pass in-side the gate, Some sweet day, some sweet day;
3. We shall meet our loved and own, Some sweet day, some sweet day;

We shall cross the storm-y tide, Some sweet day, some sweet day;
Peace and plen-ty for us wait, Some sweet day, some sweet day;
Gath-'ring round the great white throne, Some sweet day, some sweet day;

We shall press the sands of gold, While be-fore our eyes un-fold,
We shall hear the wondrous strain, Glo-ry to the Lamb that's slain;
By the tree of life so fair, Joy and rap-ture ev'-ry-where;

Heav-en's splen-dors, yet un-told, Some sweet day, some sweet day.
Christ was dead, but lives a-gain, Some sweet day, some sweet day.
O the bliss of o-ver there, Some sweet day, some sweet day.

Copyright, 1883, by D. B. TOWNER.

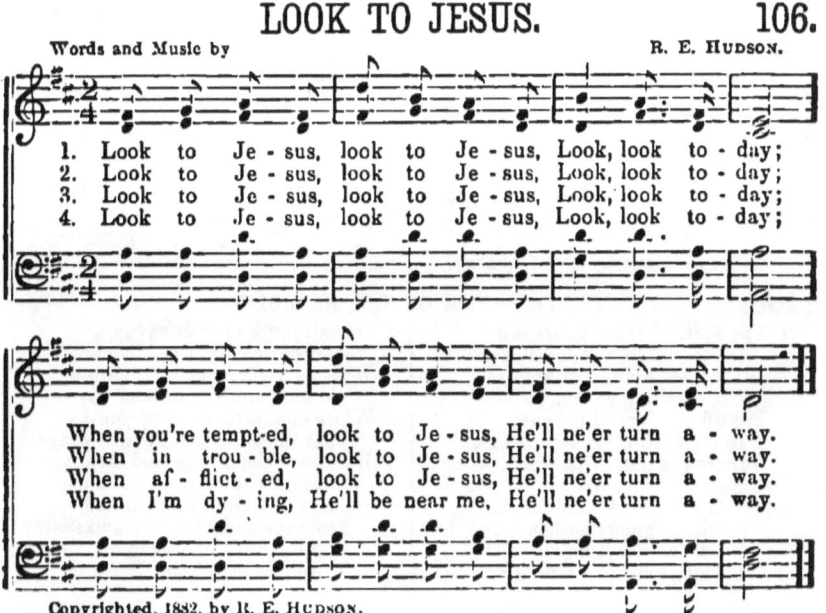

107. COLD WATER FOR ME.

Words and Music by R. E. Hudson.

1. Oh, come and join our temp'rance band, For truth and right we'll firm-ly stand, We're joined to-geth-er hand in hand, Cold wa-ter for me.
2. Cold wa-ter, pure cold wa-ter bright, Shall be our watchward day and night, We're sure to con-quer in this fight, Cold wa-ter for me.
3. We'll nev-er drink the poisoned cup, No! we'll not e-ven take a sup Of that which ru-ins, hangs men up, Cold wa-ter for me.

CHORUS.

Cold wa-ter is my mot-to, Cold wa-ter, I'm a cold wa-ter boy, Cold wa-ter is my mot-to, Cold wa-ter for me.
girl,

Copyrighted, 1882, by R. E. Hudson.

108. BATTLE HYMN OF THE REPUBLIC.

1 The light of truth is breaking,
  On the mountain-top it gleams;
  Let it flash along our valleys,
  Let it glitter on our streams,
  Till all our land awakens
  In its flush of golden beams.
  Our God is marching on.
    CHORUS.
    Glory, glory, hallelujah!
    Glory, glory, hallelujah!
    Glory, glory, hallelujah!
    Our God is marching on.

2 Our strength is in Jehovah,
  And our cause is in His care;
  With Almighty hands to help us,
  We have faith to do and dare,
  While confiding in the promise
  That the Lord will answer prayer.

3 With purpose strong and steady,
  In the great Jehovah's name,
  We rise to snatch our kindred
  From the depths of woe and shame,
  And the jubilee of freedom
  To the slaves of sin proclaim.

JESUS IS CALLING. 109.

Words and Music by R. E. HUDSON.

1. Come, ye weary and oppressed, Jesus now is calling you,
2. Tho' your sins like mountains rise, Jesus now is calling you,
3. Tho' your sins like scarlet be, Jesus now is calling you,
4. Come, ye wand'rers from the fold, Jesus now is calling you,

Come to Him, he'll give you rest, Still He bids you come.
He has made the sacrifice, Still He bids you come.
From your sins He'll set you free, Still He bids you come.
Oh, His love can ne'er be told, Still He bids you come.

CHORUS.

Jesus now is calling, calling, calling,
Jesus now is calling, calling, calling, calling, calling, calling,
Jesus now is calling you, Calling you to come.

Copyrighted, 1882, by R. E. HUDSON.

COME, YE SINNERS. 110.

1 Come, ye sinners, poor and needy,
  Weak and wounded, sick and sore;
  Jesus ready stands to save you,
  Full of pity, love, and power.

CHORUS.
  Turn to the Lord and seek salvation;
  Sound the praise of His dear name;
  Glory, honor, and salvation!
  Christ, the Lord, has come to reign.

2 Now, ye needy, come and welcome;
  God's free bounty glorify;
  True belief and true repentance,—
  Every grace that brings you nigh.

3 Let not conscience make you linger;
  Nor of fitness fondly dream;
  All the fitness He requireth
  Is to feel your need of Him!

112. KENTUCKY.

1 And can I yet delay
  My little all to give?
 To tear my soul from earth away,
  For Jesus to receive?

2 Nay, but I yield, I yield;
  I can hold out no more;
 I sink, by dying love compelled,
  And own Thee conqueror.

3 Though late, I all forsake,
  My friends, my all, resign;
 Gracious Redeemer, take, O take,
  And seal me ever thine.

4 Come, and possess me whole,
  Nor hence again remove;
 Settle and fix my wavering soul
  With all thy weight of love.

OVER THERE. 114.

1 Oh! think of the home over there,
  By the side of the river of light,
  Where the saints, all immortal and fair,
  Are robed in their garments of white.

Cho.—Over there, over there,
  Oh, think of the home over there,
  Over there, over there, over there,
  Oh, think of the friends over there.

2 Oh, think of the friends over there,
  Who before us the journey have trod,
  Of the songs that they breathe on the air,
  In their home in the palace of God.

3 My Saviour is now over there,
  There my kindred and friends are at rest;
  Then away from my sorrow and care,
  Let me fly to the land of the blest.

111. AWAKE, MY SOUL!

I. N. McHose, by per.

1. A-wake, my soul! stretch ev'-ry nerve, And press with vig-or on;
2. 'Tis God's all an-i-ma-ting voice That calls thee from on high;
3. Blest Sav-iour! in-tro-duced by thee, Our race have we be-gun;

A heav'n-ly race de-mands thy zeal, And an im-mor-tal crown.
'Tis He whose hand pre-sents the prize To thine as-pir-ing eye.
And, crowned with vic-'try, at Thy feet We'll lay our troph-ies down.

CHORUS.

A crown, a bright, im-mor-tal crown, A glit-t'ring crown I see;
'Tis mine, all mine, for-ev-er mine, If I but faith-ful be.

Copyrighted, 1885, by I. N. McHose.

112. KENTUCKY.

1 And can I yet delay
  My little all to give?
  To tear my soul from earth away,
  For Jesus to receive?

2 Nay, but I yield, I yield;
  I can hold out no more;
  I sink, by dying love compelled,
  And own Thee conqueror.

3 Though late, I all forsake,
  My friends, my all, resign;
  Gracious Redeemer, take, O take,
  And seal me ever thine.

4 Come, and possess me whole,
  Nor hence again remove;
  Settle and fix my wavering soul
  With all thy weight of love.

TAKE MY HAND, DEAR JESUS. 113.

KATE OSBORN. WM. W. BENTLEY, By per.

1. Ev-er blessed Je-sus, Listen un-to me, Bow thine ear and hear me,
2. Ever blessed Jesus, Bless Thy wayward child, Keep my feet from straying
3. Help me, blessed Jesus, Leave me not alone, Give me strength and patience,

While I call to thee; I am weak and sin-ful, Thou art pure and strong;
Through the de-sert wild; I would never wander From Thy lov-ing side,
Till each du-ty's done; And when life is ended, I Thy face would see,

CHORUS.

Take my hand, dear Je-sus, Lead thy child along.
Ev - er bless - ed Je-sus, Be my constant guide. Take my hand, dear Jesus,
Hear my pray'r, dear Jesus, Take me up to Thee.

Let me nev-er stray, Take my hand and lead me in the bet-ter way.

OVER THERE. 114.

1 Oh! think of the home over there,
  By the side of the river of light,
  Where the saints, all immortal and fair,
  Are robed in their garments of white.

Cho.—Over there, over there,
  Oh, think of the home over there,
  Over there, over there, over there,
  Oh, think of the friends over there.

2 Oh, think of the friends over there,
  Who before us the journey have trod,
  Of the songs that they breathe on the air,
  In their home in the palace of God.

3 My Saviour is now over there,
  There my kindred and friends are at rest;
  Then away from my sorrow and care,
  Let me fly to the land of the blest.

115. WAITING.

Words and Music by R. E. HUDSON.

1. Je-sus is waiting, dear sin-ner, Wait-ing to save you from sin,
2. Je-sus is seeking you, sin-ner, Seek-ing by night and by day;
3. Je-sus is knocking, my brother, Why will you turn Him a-way?

Plead-ing His blood, O how precious! Wait-ing to welcome you in.
Long-ing to hear you say welcome, Turning from all sin a-way.
Je-sus in mer-cy is pleading, Why will you longer de-lay?

CHORUS.

Wait-ing, wait-ing, Je-sus has bid-den you come;
Wait-ing, wait-ing, wand'rer, O wand'rer, come home.

Copyrighted, 1884, by R. E. HUDSON.

116. WHAT A FRIEND WE HAVE IN JESUS.

1 What a friend we have in Jesus,
  All our sins and griefs to bear!
What a privilege to carry
  Every thing to God in prayer!
Oh, what peace we often forfeit,
  Oh, what endless pain we bear—
All because we do not carry
  Every thing to God in prayer.

2 Have we trials and temptations?
  Is there trouble anywhere?
We should never be discouraged,
  Take it to the Lord in prayer;
Can we find a friend so faithful,
  Who will all our sorrows share?
Jesus knows our every weakness;
  Take it to the Lord in prayer.

GLORY TO HIS NAME! 117.

E. A. Hoffman.   Rev. J. H. Stockton, by per.

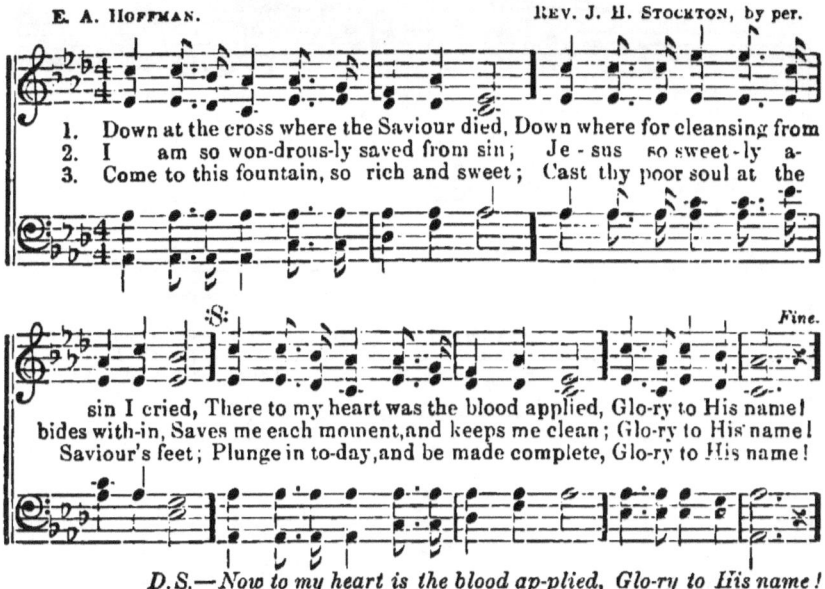

1. Down at the cross where the Saviour died, Down where for cleansing from sin I cried, There to my heart was the blood applied, Glory to His name!
2. I am so wondrously saved from sin; Jesus so sweetly abides within, Saves me each moment, and keeps me clean; Glory to His name!
3. Come to this fountain, so rich and sweet; Cast thy poor soul at the Saviour's feet; Plunge in to-day, and be made complete, Glory to His name!

D. S.—Now to my heart is the blood applied, Glory to His name!

CHORUS.

Glory to His name! Glory to His name! Glory to His name!
Glory to His name!

---

118. I NEED THEE EVERY HOUR.

1 I need Thee every hour,
   Most gracious Lord,
No tender voice like Thine
   Can peace afford.

Cho.—I need Thee, oh! I need Thee,
   Every hour I need Thee;
O bless me now, my Saviour,
   I come to Thee.

2 I need Thee every hour,
   Stay Thou near by;
Temptations lose their **power**
   When Thou art nigh.

3 I need Thee every hour:
   Teach me Thy will;
And Thy rich promises
   In me fulfill.

119. Tune—BOYLSTON.

1 A charge to keep I have,
   A God to glorify;
A never-dying soul to save,
   And fit it for the sky.

2 To serve the present age,
   My calling to fulfill,—
O may it all my powers engage,
   To do my Master's will.

3 Arm me with jealous care,
   As in thy sight to live;
And O thy servant, Lord, prepare,
   A strict account to give.

4 Help me to watch and pray,
   And on thyself rely,
Assured, if I my trust betray,
   I shall forever die.

120. JESUS, MY ALL.

1. Lord, at thy mer-cy-seat, Hum-bly I fall; Plead-ing Thy promise sweet, Lord, hear my call: Now let Thy work be-gin, Oh, make me pure with-in, Cleanse me from ev'-ry sin, Je-sus, my all.
2. Tears of re-pent-ent grief Si-lent-ly fall; Hear thou my un-be-lief, Hear Thou my call; Oh, how I pine for Thee! 'Tis all my hope, my plea, Je-sus has died for me, Je-sus, my all.
3. Wash me, and make me clean—Pure as Thou art; Each root and seed of sin Take from my heart; Make me, in thought and word, Like un-to Thee, my Lord; Then be Thy grace a-dored For-ev-er-more.

121. JESUS IS MINE.

1 Fade, fade, each earthly joy,
   Jesus is mine!
Break, every tender tie,
   Jesus is mine!
Dark is the wilderness,
Earth has no resting-place,
Jesus alone can bless,
   Jesus is mine!

2 Tempt not my soul away,
   Jesus is mine!
Here would I ever stay,
   Jesus is mine!
Perishing things of clay,
Born but for one brief day,
Pass from my heart away,
   Jesus is mine!

3 Farewell, mortality!
   Jesus is mine!
Welcome, eternity!
   Jesus is mine!
Welcome, O loved and blest!
Welcome, sweet scenes of rest!
Welcome, my Saviour's breast!
   Jesus is mine!

122. BETHANY.

1 Nearer, my God, to Thee,
   Nearer to Thee!
E'en though it be a cross
   That raiseth me;
Still all my song shall be,
Nearer, my God, to Thee,
   Nearer to Thee!

2 Though, like the wanderer,
   The sun gone down,
Darkness be over me,
   My rest a stone;
Yet in my dreams I'd be
Nearer, my God, to Thee,
   Nearer to Thee!

3 There let my way appear,
   Steps unto heaven;
All that Thou sendest me
   In mercy given;
Angels to beckon me
Nearer, my God, to Thee,
   Nearer to Thee!

126. BEAUTIFUL LAND.

ANON.

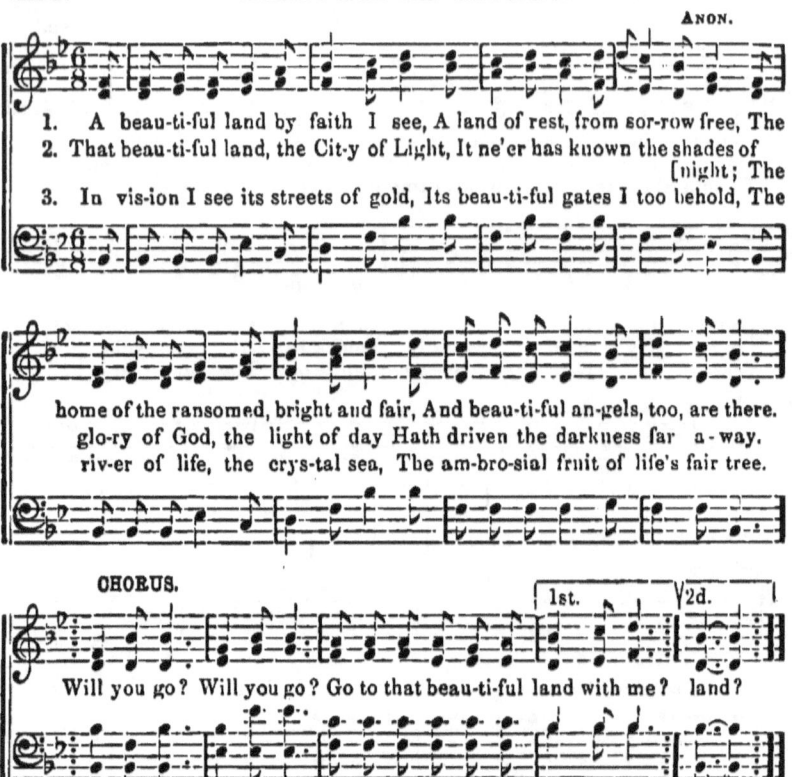

1. A beau-ti-ful land by faith I see, A land of rest, from sor-row free, The home of the ransomed, bright and fair, And beau-ti-ful an-gels, too, are there.
2. That beau-ti-ful land, the Cit-y of Light, It ne'er has known the shades of [night; The glo-ry of God, the light of day Hath driven the darkness far a-way.
3. In vis-ion I see its streets of gold, Its beau-ti-ful gates I too behold, The riv-er of life, the crys-tal sea, The am-bro-sial fruit of life's fair tree.

CHORUS.
Will you go? Will you go? Go to that beau-ti-ful land with me? land?

127. NOTHING BUT THE BLOOD.

1 What can wash away my sins?
    Nothing but the blood of Jesus!
  What can make me whole again?
    Nothing but the blood of Jesus!

CHORUS.
Oh, precious is the flow
That makes me white as snow,
No other fount I know,
Nothing but the blood of Jesus.

2 Nothing can for sin atone,
    Nothing but the blood of Jesus;
  Naught of good that I have done,
    Nothing but the blood of Jesus.

3 This is all my hope and peace,
    Nothing but the blood of Jesus;
  This is all my righteousness,
    Nothing but the blood of Jesus.

128. No. 122 Songs of Peace, Love and Joy.

1 All my life long I had panted
    For a draught from some cool spring,
  That I hoped would quench the burning
    Of the thirst I felt within.

CHORUS.
Hallelujah! I have found Him—
Whom my soul so long has craved!
Jesus satisfies my longings;
Through His blood I now am saved.

2 Feeding on the husks around me,
    Till my strength was almost gone;
  Longed my soul for something better,
    Only still to hunger on.

3 Well of water, ever springing,
    Bread of life, so rich and free;
  Untold wealth that never faileth,
    My Redeemer is to me.

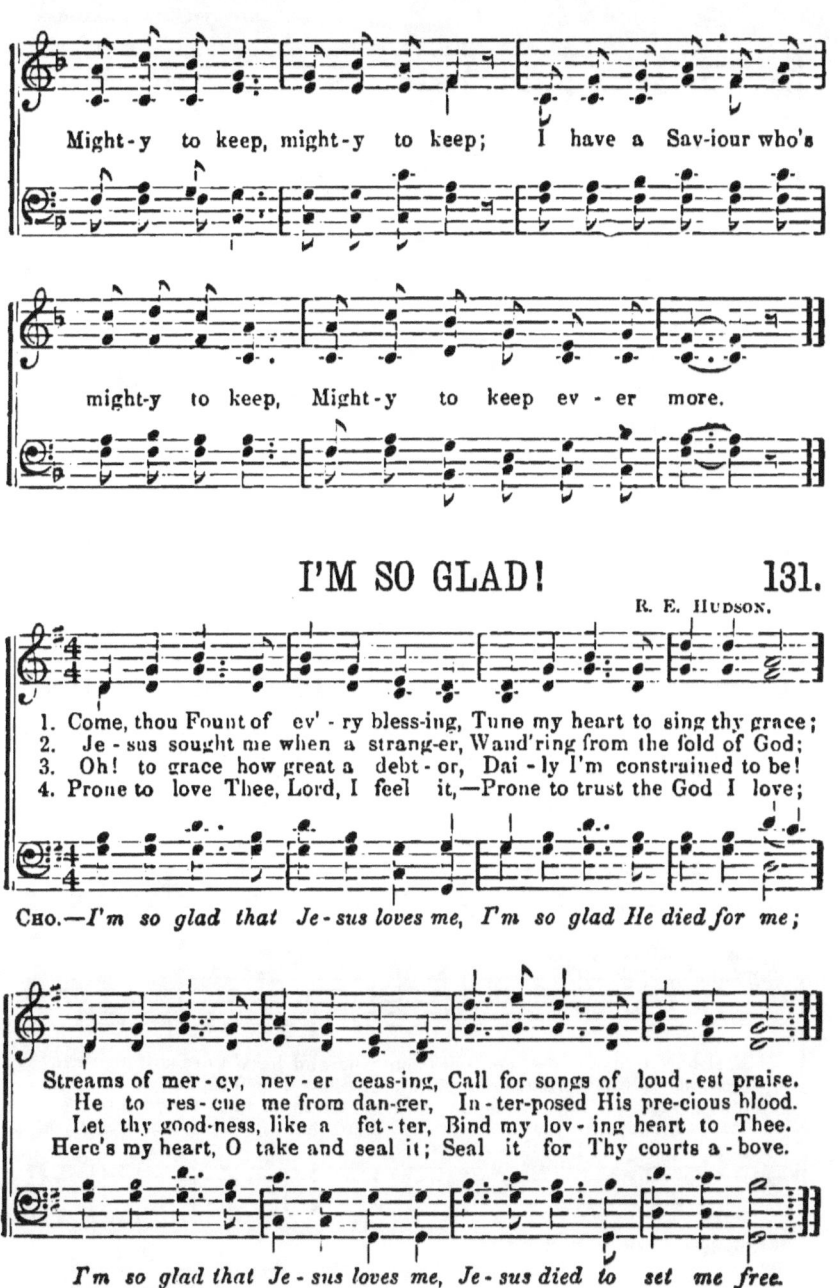

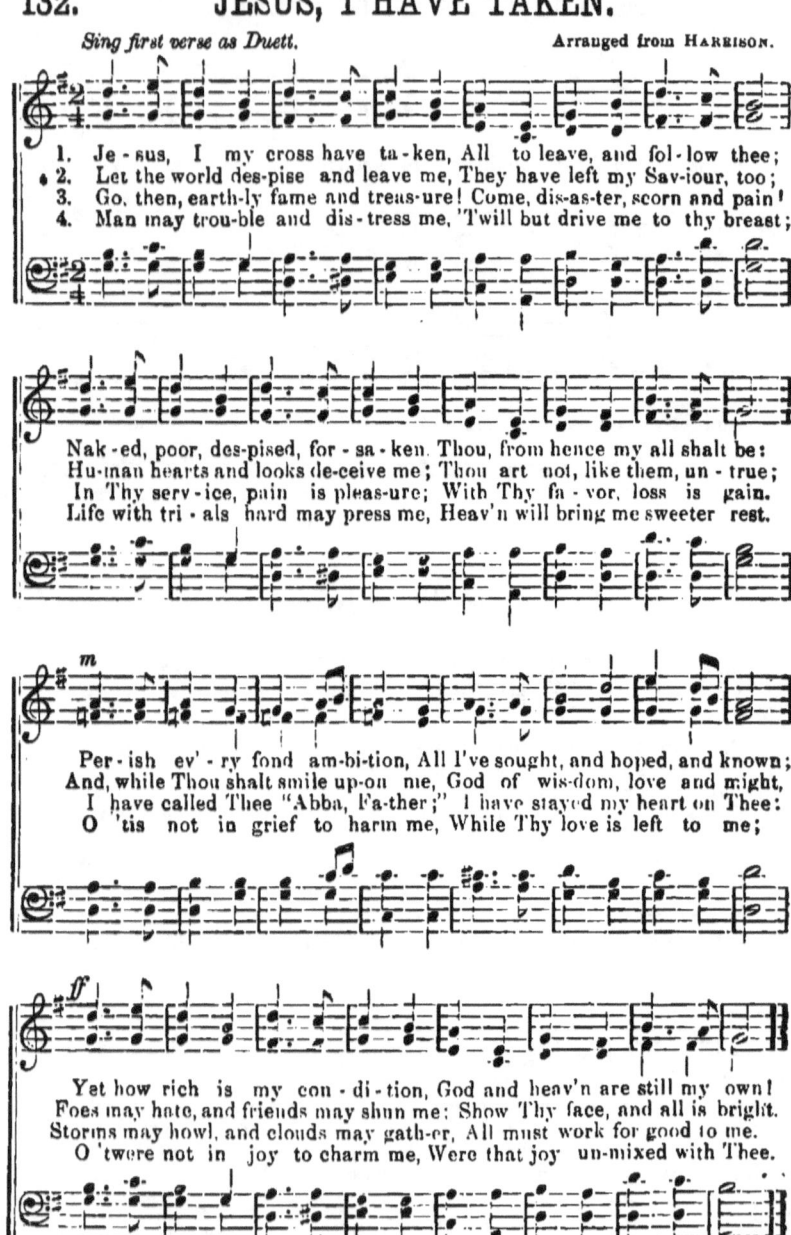

136. I'LL BE THERE.

Arranged by R. E. Hudson.

1. { On Jordan's stormy banks I stand, And cast a wishful eye
   To Canaan's fair and happy land, Where my possessions lie. }
2. { O the transporting, rapturous scene, That rises to my sight!
   Sweet fields, arrayed in living green, And rivers of delight. }
3. { There generous fruits that never fail, On trees immortal grow;
   There rock, and hill, and brook, and vale, With milk and honey flow. }
4. { O'er all those wide-extended plains Shines one eternal day;
   There God the Son forever reigns, And scatters night away. }

REFRAIN.

I'll be there, I'll be there, When the first trumpet sounds I'll be there.
I'll be there, I'll be there, I'll be there.
I'll be there, I'll be there, When the first trumpet sounds I'll be there.
Will you be there? Will you be there?

137. GATHER AT THE RIVER.

1 Shall we gather at the river,
　Where bright angel feet have trod?
With its crystal tide forever
　Flowing by the throne of God?

CHORUS.

Yes, we'll gather at the river,
The beautiful, the beautiful river,
Gather with the saints at the river,
That flows by the throne of God.

2 Ere we reach the shining river,
　Lay we every burden down,
Grace our spirit will deliver,
　And provide a robe and crown.

3 Soon we'll reach the silver river,
　Soon our pilgrimage will cease;
Soon our happy hearts will quiver,
　With the melody of peace.

138. SWEET BY-AND-BY.

1 There's a land that is fairer than day,
　And by faith we can see it afar;
For the Father waits over the way,
　To prepare us a dwelling place there.

CHORUS.

In the sweet by-and-by,
We shall meet on that beautiful shore;
In the sweet by-and-by,
We shall meet on that beautiful shore.

2 We shall sing on that beautiful shore
　The melodious songs of the blest,
And our spirits shall sorrow no more,
　Not a sigh for the blessing of rest.

3 To our bountiful Father above
　We will offer our tribute of praise,
For the glorious gift of His love, [days.
　And the blessings that hallow our

145 MUSIC No. 243.

Forever here my rest shall be,
  Close to thy bleeding side;
This all my hope and all my plea,
  For me the Savior died!

My dying Savior and my God,
  Fountain for guilt and sin,
Sprinkle me ever with thy blood
  And cleanse and keep me clean.

Wash me and make me thus thine own
  Wash me, and mine thou art;
Wash me, but not my feet alone,
  My hands, my head, my heart.

The atonement of thy blood apply,
  Till faith to sight improve;
Till hope in full fruition die.
  And all my soul be love.

146 MARCHING TO ZION. G

Come, ye, that Love the Lord,
  And let your Joys be known,
Join in a song with sweet accord,
  ||While ye surround the throne.||
Cho.—We're marching to Zion,
    Beautiful, beautiful Zion,
  We're marching upward to Zion
    The beautiful city of God.

The hill of Zion yields,
  A thousand sacred sweets,
|Before we reach the heavenly fields||
  Or walk the golden streets.

Then let our songs abound,
  And every tear be dry,   [ground||
||We're marching through Immanuels
  To fairer worlds on high.

147 THE SOLID ROCK. G

My hope is built on nothing less
Than Jesus blood and righteousness,
I dare not trust the sweetest frame,
But wholly lean on Jesus' name.
Cho.—On Christ the solid rock I stand,
  ||All other ground is sinking sand.||

When darkness seems to veil his face
I rest on his unchanging grace,
In every high and stormy gale,
My anchor holds within the veil.

His word, his covenant, and blood,
Support me in the 'whelming flood;
When all around on earth gives way,
He then is all my hope and stay.

148 WORK.

Work, for the night is coming;
Work through the morning hours
Work while the dew is sparkling;
Work 'mid springing flowers;
Work when the day grows brighter,
W rk, in the glowing sun;
Work, for the night is coming,
Woen man's work is done.

Work for the night is coming.
Work through the sunny noon;
Fill brightest hours with labor;
Rest comes sure and soon,
Give every flying minute
Something to keep in store;
Work, for the night is coming;
When man works no more.

Work, for the night is coming,
Under the sunset skies;
While the bright tints are glowing,
Work for daylight flies.
Work, till the last beam fadeth,
Fadeth to shine no more
Work, while the night is dark'ning,
When man's work is o'er.

149 MUSIC No. 348.

I would not live alway;
I ask not to stay where storm after
Rises dark o'er the way: [storm
The few lurid mornings
That dawn on us here,
Are enough for lifes joys,
Full enough for its cheer.
Cho.—Home, home sweet, sweet home
  Prepare me dear Savior for
    heaven my home.

I would not live alway;
No—welcome the tomb!
Since Jesus hath lain there
I dread not its gloom;
There sweet be my rest,
Till he bid me arise,
To hail him in triumph,
Descending the skies.

Who, who would live alway,
Away from his God—
Away from yon heaven,
That blissful abode,
Where rivers of pleasure
Flow bright o'er the plains,
And the noontide of glory
Eternally reigns?

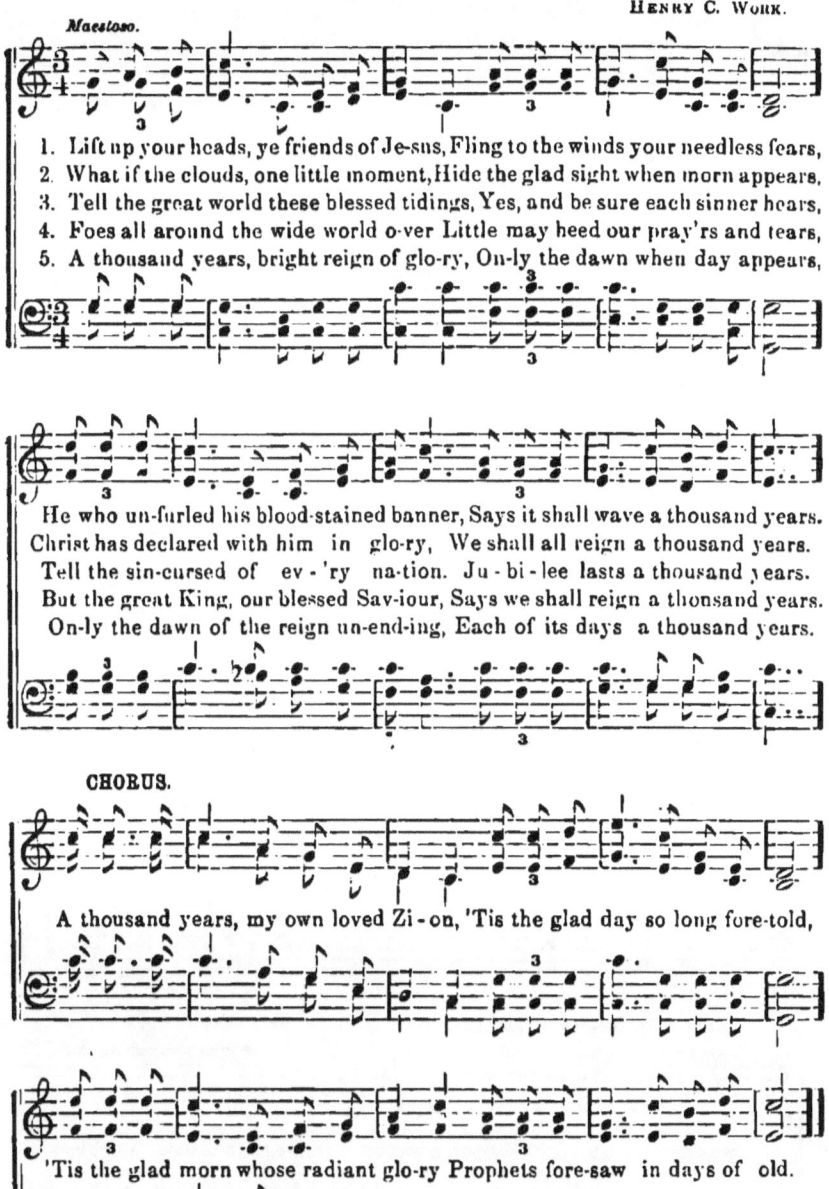

SLEEPER IN ZION, AWAKE!—Concluded.

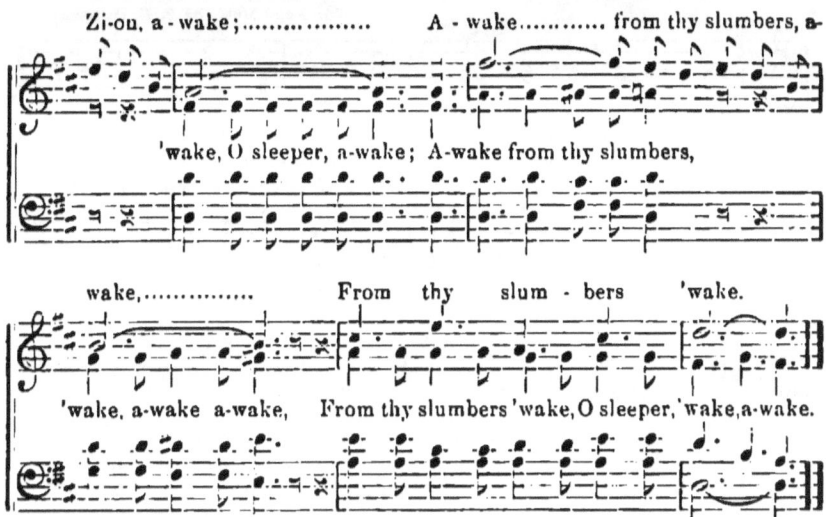

Copyrighted, 1888, by I. N. McHose.

BALM IN GILEAD. 154.

Arr. by R. E. Hudson.

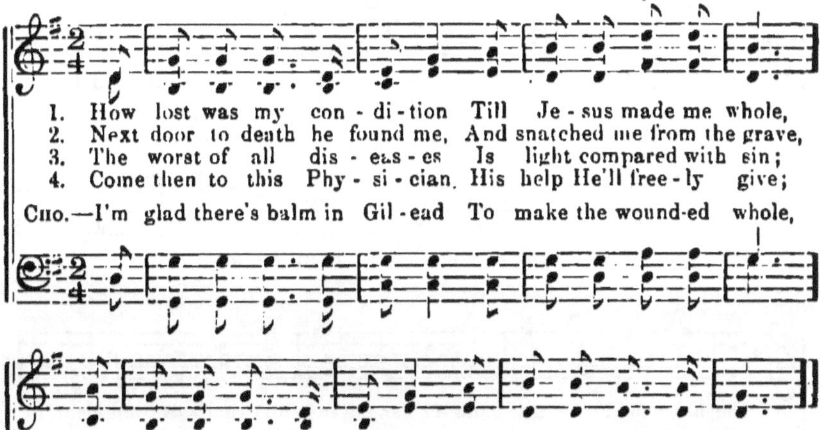

1. How lost was my con-di-tion Till Je-sus made me whole,
2. Next door to death he found me, And snatched me from the grave,
3. The worst of all dis-eas-es Is light compared with sin;
4. Come then to this Phy-si-cian, His help He'll free-ly give;

Cho.—I'm glad there's balm in Gil-ead To make the wound-ed whole,

There is but one Phy si-cian Can cure a sin-sick soul.
To tell to all a-round me His wondrous power to save.
On ev'-ry part it seiz-es, But ra-ges most with-in.
He makes no hard con-di-tion, 'Tis on-ly, Look and live.

There's pow'r e-nough in Je-sus To cure a sin-sick soul.

155. MY DREAM.

Words and Music by R. E. HUDSON.

1. I had a dream of long a-go, I heard them sing once more,
   The same old songs they used to sing In long gone days of yore.
   They sang of Him, who died for me,—How sweet it was to hear
   The old, old hymn my moth-er sang, In ac-cent soft and clear.

2. Now while they sang, poor sin-ners came With tears of sor-row cried:
   What shall I do? I heard them say, Look to the cru-ci-fied,
   Then while they prayed in Je-sus' name, That they might now be-lieve;
   I heard a shout that thrilled my soul, I do my Lord re-ceive.

3. Then each with joy be-gan to tell, Of Je-sus and his love,
   While old and young in repturous strain Would sing of joys a-bove,
   Now as the part-ing hour had come, When they must say good-by
   They joined in prayer then sang once more I'll to thy bos-som fly.

SING ONE VERSE OF NO. 156 AS FIRST CHORUS.

SING ONE VERSE OF NO. 157 AS SECOND CHORUS.

SING ONE VERSE OF NO. 158 AS THIRD CHORUS.

Copyrighted, 1884, by R. E. Hudson.

MEAR. 156.

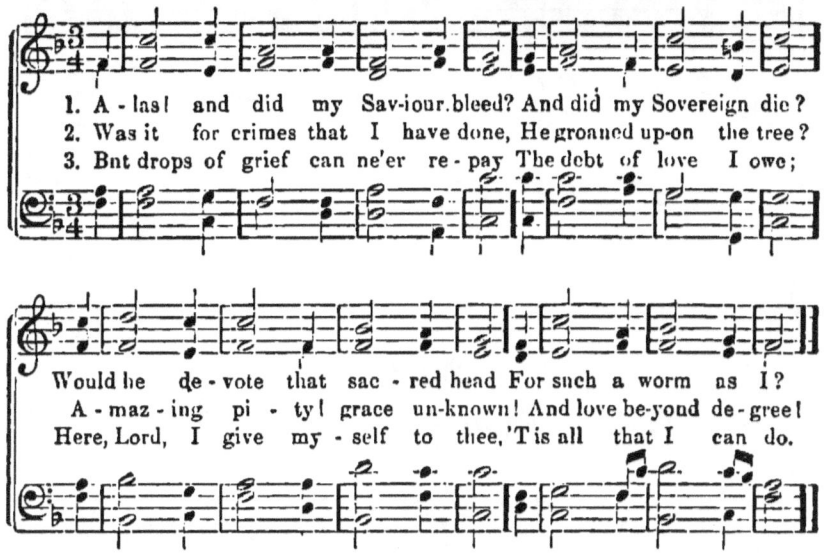

1. A-las! and did my Saviour bleed? And did my Sovereign die? Would he devote that sacred head For such a worm as I?
2. Was it for crimes that I have done, He groaned upon the tree? Amazing pity! grace unknown! And love beyond degree!
3. But drops of grief can ne'er repay The debt of love I owe; Here, Lord, I give myself to thee, 'Tis all that I can do.

HAPPY DAY. 157.

1. { O happy day, that fixed my choice On thee, my Saviour, and my God! / Well may this glowing heart rejoice, And tell its raptures all abroad. } Happy day, happy day, When Jesus wash'd my sins away! { He taught me how to watch and pray, / And live rejoicing every day;

2. 'Tis done, the great transaction's done, I am my Lord's and he is mine; He drew me, and I followed on, Charmed to confess the voice divine.

3. Now rest, my long divided heart: Fixed on this blissful centre, rest; Nor ever from thy Lord depart, With him of every good possessed.

Copyrighted, 1884, by R. E. HUDSON.

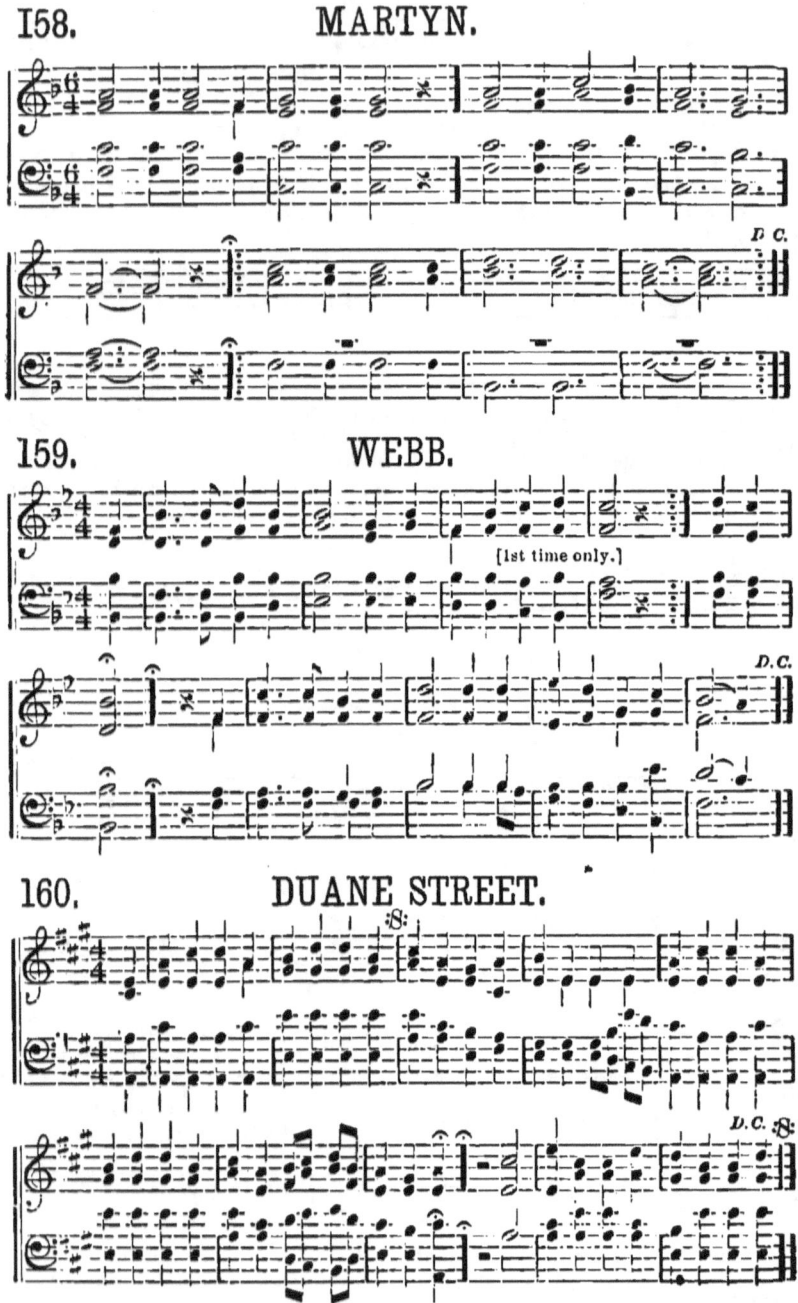

161 MUSIC No. 158.

Jesus, lover of my soul,
  Let me to thy bosom fly,
While the nearer waters roll,
  While the tempest still is high.
Hide me, oh, my Savior! hide,
  Till the storm of life is past;
Safe into the haven guide,
  Oh, receive my soul at last.

Other refuge have I none;
  Hangs my helpless soul on thee;
Leave, oh, leave me not alone!
  Still support and comfort me.
All my trust on thee is stayed;
  All my help from thee I bring;
Cover my defenceless head
  With the shadow of thy wing.

Plenteous grace with thee is found;
  Grace to cover all my sin;
Let the healing streams abound;
  Make and keep me pure within.
Thou of life the fountain art;
  Freely let me take of thee;
Spring thou up within my heart;
  Rise to all eternity.

162 MUSIC No. 159.

The morning light is breaking;
  The darkness disappears;
The sons of earth are waking
  To penitential tears;
Each breeze that sweeps the ocean
  Brings tidings from afar
Of nations in commotion,
  Prepared for zion's war.

Blest river of salvation,
  Pursue thy onward way;
Flow thou to every nation,
  Nor in thy richness stay;
Stay not till all the lowly
  Triumphant reach their home;
Stay not till all the holy
  Proclaim, "The Lord is come!"

163 MUSIC No. 160.

Of Him who did salvation bring,
  I could forever think and sing;
Arise, ye needy,—he'll relieve;
Arise, ye guilty,—he'll forgive.
Ask but his grace, and lo, 'tis given;
Ask, and he turns your hell to heav'n;
Tho' sin and sorrow wound my soul,
  Jesus, thy balm, will make it whole.

To shame our sins he blushed in blood
  He closed his eyes to show us God;
Let all the world fall down and know
That none but God such love can show
'Tis thee I love, for thee alone
  I shed my tears and make my moan;
Where'er I am, where'er I move,
  I meet the object of my love.

164 MUSIC No. 160.

He dies! the friend of sinners dies!
  Lo! Salem's daughters weep around;
A solemn darkness veils the skies,
A sudden trembling shakes the ground
Come, saints, and drop a tear or two
  For him who groaned beneath your load;
He shed a thousand drops for you.—
  A thousand drops of richer blood.

Here's love and grief beyond degree,
  The Lord of glory dies for man!
But lo! what sudden joys we see,
  Jesus, the dead, revives again!
The rising God forsakes the tomb;
  In vain the tomb forbids his rise;
Cherubic legions guard him home,
  And shout him welcome to the skies

Break off your tears, ye saints, and tell
  How high your great Deliverer reigns;
Sing how he spoiled the hosts of hell,
  And led the monster Death in chains.
Say, "Live forever, wondrous King!
  Born to redeem, and strong to save;"
Then ask the monster, "Where's thy sting?" [ing Grave?"
And, "Where's thy victory, boast-

165 WHITER THAN SNOW. A

Dear Jesus I long
  To be perfectly whole,
I want Thee forever
  To live in my soul,
Break down every idol,
  Cast out every foe,
Now wash me, and I
  Shall be whiter than snow.

Cho.—Whiter than snow,
  Yes, whiter than snow,
Now wash me, and I
  Shall be whiter than snow.

Dear Jesus, for this
  I most humbly entreat;
I wait, blessed Lord,
  At thy crucified feet,
By faith, for my cleansing,
  I see Thy blood flow,
Now wash me, and I
  Shall be whiter than snow.

170. MUSIC No. 167.

All hail the power of Jesus' name,
  Let angels prostrate fall;
Bring forth the royal diadem,
  And crown him Lord of all.

Sinners whose love can ne'er forget,
  The wormwood and the gall,
Go spread your trophies at his feet,
  And crown him Lord of all.

Let every kindred, every tribe,
  On this terrestial ball,,
To him all majesty ascribe,
  And crown him Lord of all.

Oh, that with yonder sacred throng,
  We at his feet may fall.
We'll join the everlasting song.
  And crown him Lord of all.

171. MUSIC No. 168.

The great Physician now is near,
  The sympathizing Jesus;
He speaks the drooping heart to cheer
  Oh, hear the voice of Jesus.

CHORUS.
Sweetest note in seraph song,
Sweetest Name on mortal tongue,
Sweetest carol ever sung,
  Jesus, blessed Jesus.

Your many sins are all forgiven,
  I now believe in Jesus;
Go on your way in peace to heaven,
  And wear a crown with Jesus.

All glory to the dying Lamb,
  I now believe in Jesus;
I love the blessed Savior's name,
  I love the name of Jesus.

172. MUSIC No. 169.

My body, soul and spirit,
  Jesus I give to thee,
A consecrated off'ring,
  Thine evermore to be.

CHORUS.
My all is on the alter,
  I'm waiting for the fire
Waiting, waiting, waiting,
  I'm waiting for the fire.

O, Jesus mighty Savior,
  I trust in thy great name,
I look for thy salvation,
  Thy promise now I claim.

Oh, let the fire descending,
  Just now upon my soul,
Consume my humble off'ring,
  And cleanse and make me whole.

173. I AM TRUSTING LORD. G

I am coming to the cross;
I am poor, and weak and blind;
I am counting all but dross,
I shall full salvation find.

CHO.—I am trusting, Lord in thee.
  Blest Lamb of Calvary,
  Humbly at thy cross I bow,
Jesus saves me, saves me now.

Here I give my all to thee,
Friends, and time and earthly store;
Soul and body thine to be—
Wholly thine forever more.

In thy promises I trust,
Now I feel the blood applied;
I am prostrated in the dust,
I with Christ am Crucified.

174. CLOSE TO THEE. G

Thou my everlasting portion,
More than friend or life to me,
All along my pilgrim journey,
Savior, let me walk with Thee.

CHO.—Close to thee, close to thee,
Close to Thee, close to Thee,
All along my pilgrims journey,
Savior, let me walk with Thee,

Not for ease or worldly pleasure,
Nor for fame my prayer shall be;
Gladly will I toil and suffer,
Only let me walk with Thee.

Lead me thro' the vale of shadows,
Bear me o'er lifes fitful sea.
Then the gate of life eternal,
May I enter, Lord, with Thee.

175. TAKE ME AS I AM. A

Jesus, my Lord to thee I cry,
Unless thou help me I must die;
Oh, bring thy free salvation nigh,
  And take me as I am.

CHO.—Take me as I am,
  Take me as I am,
Oh bring thy free salvation nigh,
  And take me as I am.

Helpless I am and full of guilt,
But yet for me thy blood was spilt,
And thou canst make me what thou
  But take me as I am.   [wilt,

I thirst; I long to know thy love,
Thy full salvation I would prove;
But since to thee I cannot move,
  Oh, take me as I am.

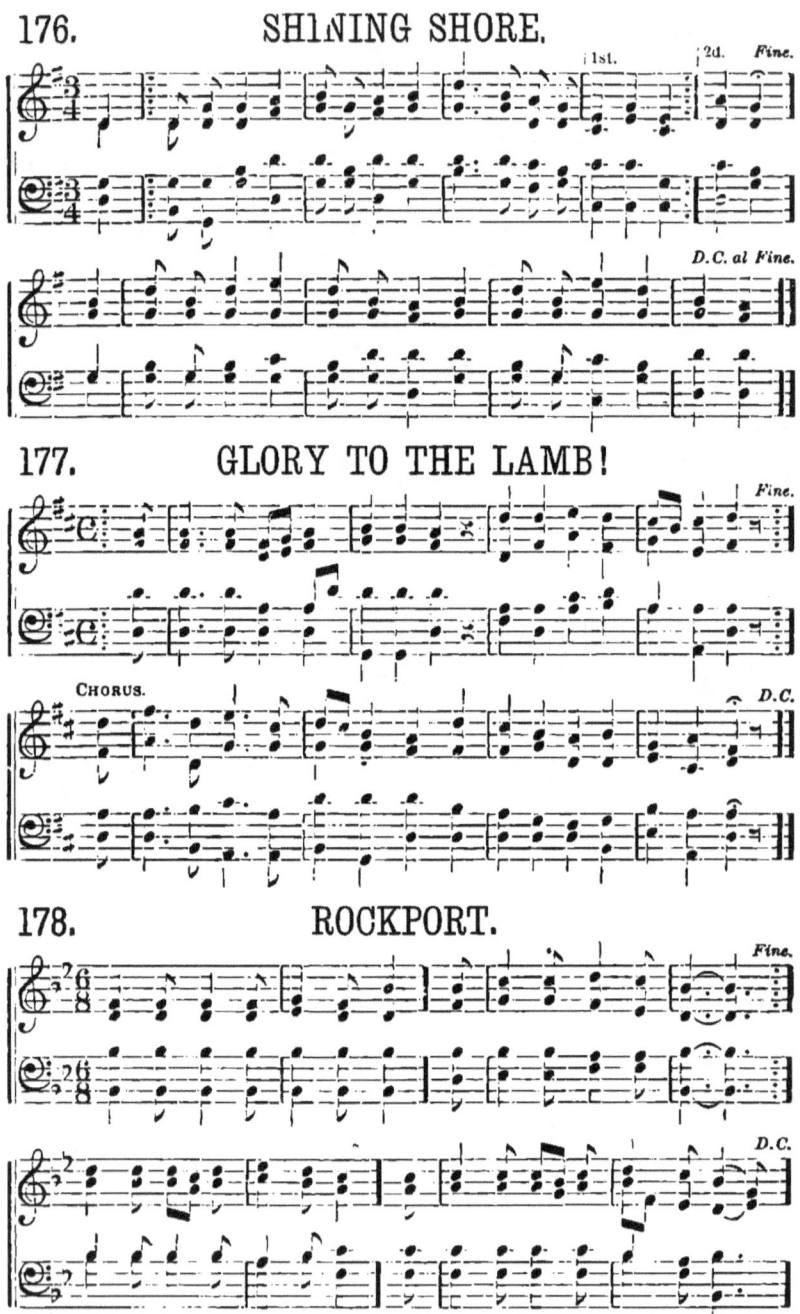

179 MUSIC No. 176.

My days are gliding swiftly by,
　And I, a pilgrim stranger,
Would not detain them as they fly,
　These hours of toil and danger.

CHORUS.

For now we stand on Jordan's strand
　Our friends are passing over;
And just before, the shining shore
　We may also discover.　　[dear
We'll gird our loins, my brethren
　Our heav'nly home discerning;
Our absent Lord has left us word,
　Let every lamp be burning.
Let sorrow's rudest tempest blow,
　Each cord on earth to sever,
Our king says come, and there's our
　Forever, O forever!　　[home.

180 MUSIC No. 177.

My savior suffered on the tree,
　Glory to the bleeding Lamb.
O come and praise the Lamb with me
　Glory to the bleeding Lamb.

CHORUS.　　[Lamb

The Lamb, the Lamb, the bleeding
　I love the sound of Jesus' name,
It sets my spirit in a flame,
　Glory to the bleeding Lamb.

He bore my sins, and curse, and shame
And I am saved thro' Jesus' name,
I know my sins are all forgiven,
And I am on my way to heaven,
And when the fighting here is o'er
I'll sing upon a happier shore.
And this my ceaseless song shall be,
That Jesus tasted death for me.

181 I AM COMING LORD. D

I hear thy welcome voice
That calls me Lord, to thee,
For cleansing in thy precious blood,
That flowed on on Calvary.

CHO.—I am coming Lord,
Coming now to thee,
Wash me, cleanse me in thy blood,
That flowed on Calvary.

Tho' coming weak and vile,
Thou dost my strength assure;
Thou dost my vileness fully cleanse,
Till spotless all and pure.

'Tis Jesus calls me on
To perfect faith and love;
To perfect hope, and peace, and trust
For earth and heaven above.

182 MUSIC No. 178.

Vain, delusive world, adieu,
　With all of creature good,
Only Jesus I pursue,
　Who bought me with his blood:
All thy pleasures I forego;
　I trample on thy wealth and pride,
Only Jesus will I know,
　And Jesus crucified.

Other knowledge I disdain;
　'Tis all but vanity,
Christ, the Lamb of God, was slain,
　He tasted death for me.
Me to save from endless woe
　The sin-atoning Victim died.
Only Jesus will I know,
　And Jesus crucified.

Him to know is life and peace,
　And pleasure without end;
This is all my happiness,
　On Jesus to depend;
Daily in his grace to grow,
　And ever in his faith abide;
Only Jesus will I know,
　And Jesus crucified.

183 NAME WRITTEN THERE A

Lord, I care not for riches,
　Neither silver nor gold,
I would make sure of heaven,
　I would enter the fold,
In the book of Thy Kingdom,
　With its pages so fair.
Tell me, Jesus, my Savior,
　Is my name written there?

CHO.—Is my name written there,
　On the page white and fair?
In the book of Thy Kingdom,
　Is my name written there?

Lord, my sins they are many,
　Like the sands of the sea,
But Thy blood, O my Savior,
　Is sufficient for me;
For thy promise is written
　In bright letters that glows,
Though your sins be as scarlet,
　I will make them like snow.

Oh, that beautiful city,
　With its mansions of light,
With its glorified beings,
　In pure garments of white,
Where no evil thing cometh,
　To despoil what is fair;
Where the angels are watching,
　Is my name written there?

187 MUSIC No. 184.

My heavenly home is bright and fair:
Nor pain nor death can enter there;
Its glittering towers the sun outshine
That heavenly mansion shall be mine.
  I'm going home, I'm going home,
  I'm going home to die no more;
  To die no more, to die no more,
  I'm going home to die no more.

My Father's house is built on high,
Far, far above the starry sky.
When from this earthly prison free,
That heavenly mansion mine shall be.

While I hear a stranger far from home,
Afflictions waves may round me foam;
Although like Lazarus, sick and poor,
My heavenly mansion is secure.

188 MUSIC No. 185.

1 Asleep in Jesus! blessed sleep,
From which none ever wake to weep!
A calm and undisturbed repose,
Unbroken by the last of foes.

2 Asleep in Jesus! O how sweet
To be for such a slumber meet!
With holy confidence to sing, [sting
That Death hath lost his venomed

3 Asleep in Jesus! peaceful rest,
Whose waking is supremely blest!
No fear, no woe shall dim that hour
That manifests the Saviors power.

4 Asleep in Jesus! O for me
May such a blissful refuge be?
Securely shall my ashes lie,
Waiting the summons from on high.

189 SWEET BY AND BY.

Let us sing of His love once again,
Of the love that can never decay,
Of the blood of the Lamb who was slain,
Till we praise him again in that day.
  ‖I believe Jesus saves
    And his blood
  Makes me whiter than snow.‖

There is cleansing and healing for all
Who will wash in the life-giving flood,
There is life everlasting and joy,
At the right hand of God through the blood.

Even now, while we taste of his love
We are filled with delight at his name
Oh, what will it be when above
We shall join in the song of the Lamb,

190 MUSIC No. 186.

I saw a happy pilgrim,
  In shining garments clad,
While traveling up the mountain.
  His countenance was glad;
He had no cares nor burdens,
  He'd laid them at the cross,
The blood of Christ, his Savior,
  Had cleansed him from all dross.
    Cho.—Then palms of victory,
      Crowns of glory,
      Palms of victory,
      We shall wear.

The summer sun was shining,
  The sweat was on his brow,
His garments worn and dusty,
  His step seemed very slow,
But he kept pressing onward,
  For he was wending home;
Still shouting as he journeyed.
  Deliverance will come:

I saw him in the evening,
  The sun was bending low,
Had overtopped the mountain;
  And reached the vale below;
He saw the golden city,,
  His everlasting home,
And shouted loud, Hosannah'
  Deliverance will come.

191 HOME OF THE SOUL. D

I will sing you a song
Of that beautiful land,
The faraway home of the soul,
Where no storms ever beat
On the glittering strand
While the years of eternity roll,
While the years of eternity roll;
Where no storms ever beat
On the glittering strand,
While the years of eternity roll.

Oh that home of the soul
In my visions and dreams,
Its bright jasper walls I can see;
:‖Till I fancy but thinly‖:
The veil intervenes
‖:Between the fair city and me,:‖

Oh how sweet it will be
In that beautiful land,
So free from all sorrow and pain;
With songs on our lips
And with harps in our hands,
‖:To meet one another again,;‖

195 MUSIC No. 192.

"Land ahead!" its fruits are waving
O'er the hills of fadeless green;
And the living waters laving
Shores where heav'nly forms are seen
Cho. Rocks and storms I fear no more
When on that eternal shore,
Drop the anchor! furl the sail!
I am safe within the veil.

Onward, bark! the cape I'm round-
See the blessed wave their hands;[ing
Hear the harps of God resounding
From the bright, immortal bands.

There, let go the anchor, riding
On this calm and silvery bay;
Sea-ward fast the tide is gliding,
Shores in sunlight stretch away.

196 MUSIC No. 193.

I love to think of heaven,
Where white robed angels are,
Where many a friend is gathered safe
From fear, and toil and care,
Cho.—There'll be no parting there,
There'll be no parting there,
In heav'n above where all is love
There'll be no parting there.

I love to think of heaven,
Where my Redeemer reigns, [rise,
Where rapturous songs of triumph
In endless, joyous strains.

I love to think of heaven,
The saints eternal home,
Where palms, and robes, and crowns
ne'er fade,
And all their joys are one.
Cho.—I'm glad salvation's free,
I'm glad salvation's free,
Salvation's free for you and me
I'm glad sal-va-tion's free.

197 HAPPY HOUR, A

O how happy are they
Who their Savior obey,
And have laid up their treasures above
Tongue cannot express
The sweet comfort and peace
Of a soul in its earliest love!

That sweet comfort was mine,
When the favor divine,
I first found in the blood of the Lamb
When my heart first believed
What a joy I received,
What a heaven in Jesus' name!

Jesus all the day long
Was my joy and my song;
Oh that all his salvation might see!
He hath loved me, I cried,
He hath suffered and died,
To redeem even rebels like me.

198 MUSIC No. 194.

I was once far away from the Sav-
And as vile as a sinner could be,[iour
I wondered if Christ the Redeemer,
Could save a poor sinner like me.

I wandered on in the darkness,
Not a ray of light could I see.
And the thought filled my heart with
[sadness,
There's no hope for a sinner like me.

I then fully trusted in Jesus,
And oh, what a joy came to me;
My heart was filled with his praises,
For saving a sinner like me.

No longer in darkness I'm walking,
For the light is now shining on me,
And now unto others I'm telling,
How he saved a poor sinner like me.

And when life's short journey is over,
And I the dear Saviour shall see,
I'll praise him forever and ever,
For saving a sinner like me.

199 TUNE—BEULAH LAND. G

I've reached the land of corn and
And all its riches freely mine ;[wine
Here shines undimmed one blissful
[day,
For all my night has passed away.
CHORUS.
O Beulah land, sweet Beulah land,
As on thy highest mount I stand,
I look away across the sea,
Where mansions are prepared for me
And view the shining glory shore,
My heav'n, my home forevermore.

The Saviour comes and walks with me
And sweet communion here have we;
He gently leads me with His hand,
For this is heaven's border land.

A sweet perfume upon the breeze
Is borne from evey vernal tree,
And flowers that never fading grow
Where streams of life forever flow.

The zephyrs seem to float to me,
Sweet sounds of heaven's melody,
As angels with the white robed throng
Join in the sweet redemption song.

203 MUSIC No. 200.

Come, O my God the promise seal,
  This mountain, sin, remove;
Now in my waiting soul reveal
  The virtue of thy love.
Cho.—I can, I will, I do believe,
    I can, I will, I do believe,
    I can, I will, I do believe,
    That Jesus saves me now.

I want thy life, thy purity,
  Thy righteousness, brought in:
I ask, desire and trust in thee,
  To be redeemed from sin

Savior, to thee my soul looks up,
  My present Savior thou!
In all the confidence of hope,
  I claim the blessing now.

204 MUSIC No. 201.

O, now I see the crimson wave,
The fountain deep and wide;
Jesus, my Lord, mighty to save,
Points to his wounded side.
Cho.—The cleansing stream, I see, I see
I plunge, and O it cleanseth me;
O, praise the Lord it cleanseth me,
It cleanseth me, yes cleanseth me.

I see the new creation rise,
I hear the speaking blood,
It speaks, polluted nature dies,
Sinks neath the cleansing flood.

I rise to walk in heaven's own light,
Above the world and sin,   [white
With hearts made pure and garments
And Christ enthroned within.

205 PISGAH.   A

When I can read my title clear
  To mansions in the skies,
I'll bid farewell to every fear,
  And wipe my weeping eyes.
Should earth against my soul engage
  And fiery darts be hurled,
Then I can smile at Satan's rage,
  And face a frowning world.

Let cares like a wild deluge come—
  Let storms of sorrow fall—
So I but safely reach my home,
  My God, my heaven, my all.
There I shall bathe my weary soul
  In seas of heavenly rest,
And not a wave of trouble roll,
  Across my peaceful breast.

206 MUSIC No. 202.

Savior breathe an evening blessing,
  Ere repose our spirits seal;
Sin and want we come confessing;
  Thou canst save and thou canst heal
Though destruction walk around us,
  Though the arrows past us fly,
Angel guards from thee surround us;
  We are safe, if thou art nigh.

Though the night be dark and dreary
  Darkness cannot hide from thee;
Thou art he who, never weary,
  Watchest where thy people be. [us
Should swift death this night o'ertake
  And our couch become our tomb
May the morn in heaven awake us,
  Clad in light and deathless bloom.

207 MUSIC No. 202.

Silently the shades of evening,
  Gather round my lowly door;
Silently they bring before me
  Faces I shall see no more.
O, the lost, the unforgotten,
  Though the world be oft forgot.
O, the shrouded and the lonely,
  In our hearts they perish not.

Living in the silent hours,
  Where our spirits only blend,
They, unlinked with earthly troubles
  We, still hoping for its end.

208 OH HOW I LOVE JESUS. A

Jesus, the name high over all,
  In hell, on earth, or sky;
Angels and men before it fall,
  And devils fear and fly.
Cho.—O, how I love Jesus;
    O, how I love Jesus;
    O, how I Love Jesus,
    Because he first loved me.

Jesus, the name to sinners dear,—
  The name to sinners given;
It scatters all their guilty fear,
  It turns their hell to heaven.

O that the world might taste and see,
  The riches of his grace;
The arms of love that compass me,
  Would all mankind embrace.

212 MUSIC No. 209.

Come, every soul, by sin oppressed,
 There's mercy with the Lord,
And he will surely give you rest,
 By trusting in his word.
Cho.—Only trust him, only trust him
 Only trust him now;
He will save you, he will save you,
 He will save you now.

For Jesus shed his precious blood
 Rich blessings to bestow;
Plunge now into the crimson tide
 That washes white as snow.

Yes, Jesus is the Truth, the Way,
 That leads you into rest,
Believe in him without delay,
 And you are fully blest.

213 MUSIC No. 210.

In evil long I took delight,
 Unawed by shame or fear,
'Till a new object met my sight,
 And stopped my wild career.
Cho.—O, the Lamb, the bleeding Lamb
 The Lamb upon Calvary,
The Lamb that was slain, [for me.
 That liveth again, to intercede

I saw one hanging on a tree,
 In agonies and blood,
Who fixed his anguid eyes on me,
 As near his cross I stood.

Sure never till my latest breath
 Can I forget that look;
It seemed to charge me with his death
 Though not a word he spoke.

My conscience felt and own'd the guilt
 And plunged me in despair;
I saw my sins his blood had spilt,
 And helped to nail him there.

214 MUSIC No. 211.

We praise thee, O God,
 For the Son of thy love,
For Jesus who died,
 And is now gone above.
Cho.—Hallelujah! thine the glory,
 Hallelujah! amen.‖
 Revive us again.

We praise thee, O God,
 For thy Spirit of light,
Who has shown us our Savior,
 And scattered our night.

All glory and praise,
 To the Lamb that was slain,
Who has born all our sins,
 And has cleansed every .tain.

215 WE SHALL MEET HIM. A

The prize is set before us,
 To win, His words implore us,
The eye of God is o'er us
 From on high;
His loving tones are calling
While sin is dark, apalling,
"Tis Jesus gently calling,
 He is nigh.
Cho.—By and by we shall meet Him,
By and by we shall meet Him,
And with Jesus reign in glory,
 By and by.
By and by we shall meet Him,
By and by we shall meet Him,
And with Jesus reign in glory,
 By and by.

We'll follow where He leadeth,
We'll pasture where he feedeth,
We,ll yield to him who pleadeth
 From on high.
Then naught from Him shall sever,
Our hopes shall brighten ever,
And faith shall fail us never,
 He is nigh.

216 YIELD NOT. F

Yield not to temptation,
 For yielding is sin,
Each victory will help you
 Some other to win;
Fight manfully onward,
 Dark passions subdue,
Look ever to Jesus,
 He'll carry you through.
Cho.—Ask the Savior to help you,
 Comfort strengthen and keep you,
He is willing to aid you,
 And he will carry you through.

Shun evil companions,
 Bad language disdain,
God's name hold in reverence,
 Nor take it in vain;
Be thoughtful and earnest,
 Kind-hearted and true,
Look ever to Jesus,
 He'll carry you through.

To him that overcometh,
 God giveth a crown,
Thro' faith we shall conquer,
 Though often cast down;
He, who is our Savior,
 Our strength will renew,
Look ever to Jesus,
 He will carry you through.

220 MUSIC No. 217.

Hail, thou once dispised Jesus,
  Hail, thou Galilean King,
Thou didst suffer to release us;
  Thou didst free salvation bring,
Hail, thou agonizing Savior,
  Bearer of our sin and shame,
By thy merits we find favor,
  Life is given through thy name

Jesus, hail, enthroned in glory,
  There forever to abide;
All the heavenly hosts adore thee,
  Seated at thy Father's side;
There for sinners thou art pleading
  There thou dost our place prepare;
Ever for us enterceding,
  Till in glory we appear.

Worship, honor, power and blessing,
  Thou art worthy to receive;
Loudest praises, without ceasing,
  Meet it is for us to give,
Help, ye bright angelic spirits,
  Bring your sweetest, noblest lays;
Help to sing our Savior's merits;
  Help to chant Immanuel's praise.

221 MUSIC No. 218.

Hark, the voice of Jesus crying,
  "Who will go and work to-day?
Fields are white and harvest waiting,
  Who will bear the sheaves away?"
Loud and strong the master calleth;
  Rich reward he offers thee;
Who will answer gladly saying,
  "Here am I; take me, take me."

Let none hear you idly saying,
  "There is nothing 1 can do,"
While the souls of men are dying,
  And the master calls for you.
Take the task he gives you gladly;
  Let his work your pleasure be;
Answer quickly when he calleth,
  "Here am 1, send me, send me!"

222 MUSIC No. 156.

Come Holy spirit, heavenly Dove,
  With all thy quick'ning powers,
Kindle a flame of sacred love
  In these cold hearts of ours.

Father, and shall we ever live
  At this poor dying rate—
Our love so faint, so cold to thee,
  And thine to us so great.

Come, Holy Spirit, heavenly Dove,
  With all thy quick'ning powers,
Come, shed abroad a Savior's love,
  And that shall kindle ours.

223 MUSIC No. 219.

Just as 1 am without one plea,
But that thy blood was shed for me.
And that thou bid'st me come to thee
O, Lamb of God, 1 come, 1 come!

Just as 1 am, and waiting not
To rid my soul of one dark blot, [spot
To thee whose blood can cleanse each
O, Lamb of God, 1 come, 1 come!

Just as 1 am, thou wilt receive,
Wilt welcome, pardon, cleanse, relieve,
Because thy promise 1 believe.
O Lamb of God, 1 come, 1 come!

Just as 1 am, thy love unknown,
Has broken every barrier down;
Now to be thine, yea, thine alone,
O Lamb of God, I come!

224 MUSIC No. 237.

Lord, 1 am thine, entirely thine,
Purchased and saved by blood divine
With full consent thine I would be,
And own thy sovereign right in me.

Grant one poor sinner more a place
Among the children of thy grace;
A wretched sinner, lost to God,
But ransomed by Immanuel's blood.

Thine would 1 live, thine would 1 die
Be thine through all eternity;
The vow is past beyond repeal,
And now 1 set the solemn seal.

Here, at the cross where flows the blood
That bought my guilty soul for God,
Thee, my new Master, now 1 call,
And concentrate to thee my all.

225. NUSIC No. 218.

Love Divine all love excelling,
Joy of heaven to earth come down;
Fix in us thy humble dwelling,
All thy faithful mercies crown;
Jesus thou art all compassion,—
Pure, unbounded love thou art;
Visit us with thy salvation;
Enter ever trembling heart.

Come, almighty to deliver,
Let us all thy life receive;
Suddenly return, and never,
Never more thy temples leave;
Thee we would be always blessing,
Serve thee as thy hosts above,
Pray and praise thee without ceasing
Glory in thy perfect love.

229 MUSIC No. 226

My faith looks up to thee,
Thou Lamb of Calvary,
   Savior divine;
Now hear me while I pray,
Take all my guilt away,
O let me from this day
   Be wholly thine.

May thy rich grace impart
Strength to my fainting heart,
   My zeal inspire;
As thou hast died for me,
O may my love to thee
Pure, warm, and changeless be—
   A living fire.

While life's dark maze I tread,
And griefs around me spread,
   Be thou my guide;
Bid darkness turn to day,
Wipe sorrow's tears away,
Nor let me ever stray
   From thee aside.

230 MUSIC No. 226.

My country! 'tis of thee,
Sweet land of liberty,
   Of thee I sing;
Land where my fathers died!
Land of the pilgrim's pride!
From every mountain side
   Let freedom ring!

My native country thee,
Land of the noble, free,
   Thy name I love;
I love thy rocks and rills,
Thy woods and templed hills:
My heart with rapture thrills
   Like that above.

Our fathers' God! to thee,
Author of liberty,
   To thee we sing;
Long may our land be bright
With freedom's holy light;
Protect us by thy might,
   Great God, our King!

231 MUSIC No. 228.

Holy Spirit, faithful Guide,
Ever near the Christian's side,
Gently lead us by the hand,
Pilgrims in a desert land.
Weary souls fore'er rejoice,
While they hear that sweetest voice,
Whisp'ring softly, wanderer, come!
Follow me, I'll guide thee home.
Ever present, truest friend,
Ever near, thine aid to lend,
Leave us not to doubt and fear,
Groping on in darkness drear.
When the storms are raging sore,
Hearts grow faint and hopes give o'er
Whisper softly, wanderer, come!
Follow me, I'll guide thee home.

232 MUSIC No. 227.

How sweet the name of Jesus sounds
   In a believer's ear!
It soothes his sorrow, heals his wounds
   And drives away his fear.

It makes the wounded spirit whole,
   And calms the troubled breast;
'Tis manna to the hungry soul,
   And to the weary rest.

Till then I would thy love proclaim
   With every fleeting breath;
And may the music of Thy name
   Refresh my soul in death.

233 MUSIC No. 227.

Oh for a faith that will not shrink,
   Though pressed by every foe,
That will not tremble on the brink
   Of any earthly woe;— [clear
A faith that shines more bright and
   When tempests rage without;
That when in danger knows no fear,
   In darkness feels no doubt;—

A faith that keeps the narrow way
   Till life's last hour is fled,
And with a pure and heavenly ray
   Illumes a dying bed.

234 MUSIC No. 227.

O for a closer walk with God,
   A calm and heavenly frame;
A light to shine upon the road
   That leads me to the Lamb!

Where is the blessedness I knew,
   When first I saw the Lord?
Where is the soul-refreshing view
   Of Jesus and his word?

Return, O holy dove, return,
   Sweet messenger of rest!
I hate the sins that made thee mourn
   And drove thee from my breast.

The dearest idol I have known,
   Whate'er that idol be.
Help me to tear it from my throne,
   And worship only thee.

238 MUSIC No. 235.

Joy to the world! the Lord is come;
  Let earth receive her King;
Let every heart prepare him room,
  And heaven and nature sing.

Joy to the world! the Savior reigns;
  Let men their songs employ;
While fields and floods, rocks, hills and
  Repeat the sounding joy. [plains,

No more let sin and sorrow grow,
  Nor thorns infest the ground;
He comes to make his blessings flow
  Far as the curse is found.

He rules the world with truth and
  And makes the nations prove [grace
The glories of his righteousness,
  And wonders of his love.

239 MUSIC No. 235.

Come, let us join our cheerful songs
  With angels round the throne;
Ten thousand thousand are their
  But all their joys are one. [tongues,

"Worthy the Lamb that died," they
  "To be exalted thus!" [cry,
"Worthy the Lamb!" our hearts reply,
  "For he was slain for us."

Jesus is worthy to receive
  Honor and power divine;
And blessings more than we can give,
  Be, Lord, forever thine.

The whole creation join in one,
  To bless the sacred name
Of him that sits upon the throne,
  And to adore the Lamb.

240 MUSIC No. 236.

Arise, my soul, arise;
  Shake off thy guilty fears;
The bleeding sacrifice
  In my behalf appears;
Before the throne my surety stands,
My name is written on his hands.

He ever lives above
  For me to intercede,
His all-redeeming love,
  His precious blood to plead;
His blood atoned for all our race,
And sprinkles now the throne of
  grace.

The Father hears him pray,
  His dear annointed one;
He can not turn away
  The presence of his Son;
His Spirit answers to the blood,
And tells me I am born of God.

My God is reconciled;
  His pard'ning voice I hear;
He owns me for his child;
  I can no longer fear;
With confidence I now draw nigh,
And Father, Abba, Father, cry.

241 MUSIC No. 236.

Blow ye the trumpet, blow,
  The gladly solemn sound;
Let all the nations know,
  To earth's remotest bound,
The year of jubilee is come;
Return, ye ransomed sinners, home.

Jesus, our great High Priest,
  Hath full atonement made;
Ye weary spirits, rest;
  Ye mournful souls, be glad;
The year of jubilee is come;
Return, ye ransomed sinners, home.

Extol the Lamb of God,—
  The all-atoning Lamb;
Redemption in his blood
  Throughout the world proclaim;
The year of jubilee is come;
Return, ye ransomed sinners, home.

242 MUSIC No. 237.

While life prolongs its precious light,
  Mercy is found and peace is given;
But soon, ah, soon, approaching night
  Shall blot out every hope of heaven.

While God invites, how blest the day!
  How sweet the Gospel's charming
    sound!
Come, sinners, haste, O haste away,
  While yet a pardoning God is found.

Soon, borne on time's most rapid wing,
  Shall death command you to the
    grave,
Before his bar your spirit bring.
  And none be found to hear or save.

In that lone land of deep despair,
  No Sabbath's heavenly light shall rise.
No God regard your bitter prayer,
  No Savior call you to the skies.

243 MUSIC No. 237.

Praise God, from whom all blessings
  flow;
Praise him, all creatures here below;
Praise him above, ye heavenly host;
Praise Father, Son and Holy Ghost!

246 MUSIC No. 243.

When all thy mercies, O my God,
 My rising soul surveys,
Transported with the view, I'm lost
 In wonder, love, and praise.

When in the slippery paths of youth,
 With heedless steps I ran,
Thine arm, unseen, conveyed me safe,
 And led me up to man.

Through every period of my life
 Thy goodness I'll pursue;
And after death, in distant worlds,
 The pleasing theme renew.

Through all eternity to thee
 The grateful song I'll raise;
But O, eternity's too short
 To utter all thy praise.

247 MUSIC No. 244.

Blest be the tie that binds
 Our hearts in Christian love;
The fellowship of kindred minds
 Is like to that above.

Before our Father's throne
 We pour our ardent prayers;
Our fears, our hopes, our aims are one
 Our comforts and our cares.

We share our mutual woes,
 Our mutual burdens bear,
And often for each other flows
 The sympathizing tear.

When we asunder part
 It gives us inward pain,
But we shall still be joined in heart,
 And hope to meet again.

243 MUSIC No. 244.

My soul, be on thy guard;
 Ten thousand foes arise;
The hosts of sin are pressing hard
 To draw the from the skies.

Oh, watch, and fight, and pray;
 The battle ne'er give o'er;
Renew it boldly every day,
 And help divine implore.

Ne'er think the vict'ry won,
 Nor lay thine armor down;
The work of faith will not be done,
 Till thou obtain the crown.

Then persevere till death
 Shall bring thee to thy God;
He'll take thee, at thy parting breath,
 To his divine abode.

249 TOPLADY B

1 Rock of Ages cleft for me,
 Let me hide myself in thee
Let the water and the blood,
 From thy wounded side which flow'd
Be of sin the double cure;
 Save from wrath, and make me pure.

2 Could my tears forever flow—
 Could my zeal no languor know—
These for sin could not atone;
 Thou must save and thou alone;
In my hand no price I bring;
 Simply to thy cross I cling.

3 While I draw this fleeting breath,
 When my eyes shall close in death,
When I rise to worlds unknown,
 And behold thee on thy throne—
Rock of Ages, cleft for me,
 Let me hide myself in thee.

250 MUSIC No. 245.

Show pity, Lord, O Lord forgive!
 Let a repenting rebel live;
Are not thy mercies large and free?
 May not a sinner trust in thee

My crimes are great, but can't surpass
 The power and glory of thy grace;
Great God, thy nature hath no bound,
 So let thy pardoning love be found.

Oh wash my soul from every sin,
 And make my guilty conscience clean
Here on my heart the burden lies,
 And past offenses pain my eyes.

Yet save a trembling sinner Lord,
 Whose hope still hov'ring round
  thy word,   [there,
Would light on some sweet promise
 Some sure support against despair.

251 MUSIC No. 245.

O that my load of sin were gone!
 O that I could at last submit,
At Jesus' feet to lay it down—
 To lay my soul at Jesus' feet.

Break off the yoke of inbred sin,
 And fully set my spirit free;
I can not rest till pure within,—
 Till I am wholly lost in thee.

Fain would I learn of thee, my God;
 Thy light and easy burden prove;
The cross all stain'd with hallow'd
 The labor of thy dying love. [blood,

I would, but thou must give the power;
 My heart from every sin release;
Bring near, bring near the joyful hour
 And fill me with thy perfect peace.

WHO'LL ENLIST?—Concluded.

conflicts He will guide, He has never lost a battle, fear no more. fear no more.

Copyrighted, 1888, by R. E. Hudson.

'TWAS RUM. 253.

Words and Music by R. E. Hudson.

1. I heard a weeping mother say, While coming from the grave,
2. Once he was pure and innocent, The pride and joy of home,
3. O pity broken-hearted ones, And teach the boys to shun

Of one, to her as dear as life, She tried, but could not save.
But see the demon in the glass! At last the deed is done.
The road that leads to cruel death By rum, foul demon, rum.

CHORUS.

"'Twas rum that spoiled my darling boy, They caught him in the snare;

'Twas rum that spoiled my darling boy, I pray you, boys, beware!"

Copyrighted, 1886, by R. E. Hudson.

256. WHEN WE ARRIVE AT HOME.

Words and Music by R. E. HUDSON.

1. There's a crown for ev'-ry head, And there's joy for ev'-ry heart,
2. There's a joy in trust-ing here, And there's love with-out a fear,
3. Oh, come and join our band, For right and truth we'll stand,

CHORUS. At the end of our jour-ney, We'll re-ceive a crown,

Joy for ev'-ry heart, joy for ev'-ry heart, Who will
Love with-out a fear, love with-out a fear; Re-joic-
Right and truth we'll stand, right and truth we'll stand Till right

Bright and gold-en crown, nev-er fad-ing crown, At the

in His vine-yard en-ter, And brave-ly do
ing ev-er-more Un-til the con-
shall con-quer wrong; Then we'll join the

end of our jour-ney We'll re-ceive

his part Till we ar-rive at home?
flict's o'er And we ar-rive at home.
washed throng, When we ar-rive at home.

a crown, When we ar-rive at home.

Copyrighted, 1884, by R. E. Hudson.

SING OF HIS LOVE.—Concluded.

Copyrighted, 1895, by R. E. Hudson.

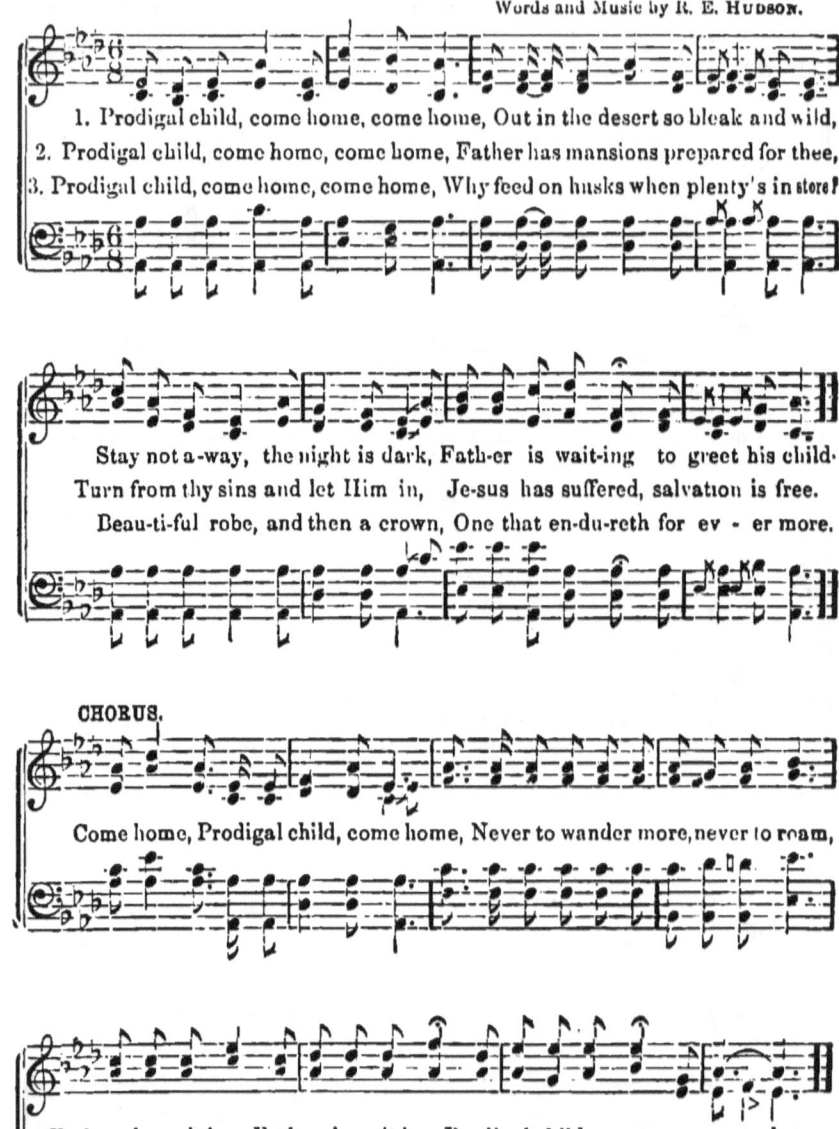

275. REWARDED.

Words and Music by R. E. HUDSON.

1. Hark, hark! son and daughter; Hear Jesus, He speaketh; Go work in the vineyard while yet it is day; The night soon will come, Your la-bor be ended; Go work for the Mas-ter, and toil while you may.
2. Think not of the con-flict, For Je-sus will lead you; The har-vest is white, and the work must be done, Oh, now heed the call, And go to the vineyard, For soon He will call you, come home, child, come home!
3. Go speak to thy broth-er, And tell him of Je-sus; Go raise up the fall-en, and tell of His love; Cheer up the faint-heart-ed, And point to the mansions pre-pared for the faith-ful in heav-en a-bove.
4. Toil on, happy child, Soon thy work will be ended; Bring sheaves thou hast gather'd, and lay at His feet; Then hear Him say, come! Well done, faith-ful ser-vant! Come sit on my throne, let thy joys be re-plete.

CHORUS.

Here I'm rewarded, there I'm rewarded, Here, and up yonder, as we gath-er round the throne; On-ly rewarded, on-ly rewarded, I'll be reward-ed for what I have done.

Copyrighted, 1882, by R. E. HUDSON.

I'VE BEEN REDEEMED. 280.

3 Come to the crimson flowing tide,
O weary, sin-sick soul!
Come, have the precious blood applied,
And it will make you whole.—Cho

4 And when we reach the "shining shore"
Amid the blood-washed throng,
We'll praise the Lamb forever more,
And this shall be our song:—Cho.

BEAUTIFUL HANDS.—Concluded.

are these ag - ed, wrinkled hands Most beauti - ful to me.
think how these hands rest-ed not When mine were at their play.
'neath the dai - sies, cold and white, These hands will folded be.
where the old grow young a - gain, I'll clasp my mother's hands.

MY AIN COUNTRIE. 282.

Miss M. A. Lee.   Scotch Song.

1. I am far frae my hame, an' I'm wea - ry af-tenwhiles, For the
I'll . . . ne'er be fu' content, un - til my e'en do see, The
D.C. But these sichts an' these soun's will as naething be to me, When I

lang'd-for hame-bringing, an' my Father's welcome smiles,
gowden gates of heav'n an' my (OMIT. . . . . . ain coun - trie.
hear the angels singing in my (OMIT. . . . . . ain coun - trie.

The earth is fleck'd wi' flow-ers, mon - y - tinted, fresh and gay;
The bird - ies war - ble blithely, for my Father's made them sae;

2 I've his gude word of promise that some gladsome day the King,
To his ain royal palace, his banished hame, will bring
Wi' een, an' wi' heart running owre we shall see
"The King in his beauty," an' our ain countrie.
My sins hae been mony, and my sorrows hae been sair,
But there they'll never vex me, nor be remembered mair.
For his bluid hath made me white, and his hand shall dry my e'e,
When he brings me hame at last to my ain countrie.

3 Like a bairn to its mither, a wee birdie to its nest,
I wad fain be ganging noo unto my Saviour's breast,
For he gathers in his bosom witless, worthless lambs like me,
An' "he carries them himsel'," to his ain countrie.
He's faithfu' that hath promised, he'll surely come again,
He'll keep his tryst wi' me, at what hour I dinna ken;
But he bids me still to wait, an' ready aye to be,
To gang at ony moment to my ain countrie.

HE'S KING OF KINGS. 286.

Respectfully dedicated to Rev. P. H. Cramper and wife.

R. E. Hudson.

1. All hail the pow'r of Jesus' name, Let angels prostrate fall;
2. Sinners! whose love can ne'er forget The wormwood and the gall;
3. Let ev'ry kindred, ev'ry tribe, On this terrestrial ball,
4. O! that with yonder sacred throng We at His feet may fall;

Bring forth the royal diadem, And crown Him Lord of all.
Go, spread your trophies at His feet, And crown Him Lord of all.
To Him all majesty ascribe, And crown Him Lord of all.
We'll join the everlasting song, And crown Him Lord of all.

CHORUS.

He's King of Kings! He's Lord of Lords! He's the morning Star, The First and the Last, No man can do the work like Him. Him.

Ritard........... 1st. 2d.

Copyrighted, 1888, by R. E. Hudson.

DISTURB NOT MY DREAMING—Concluded.

THE BETTER WISH. 291.

HENRY RUSSELL.

Robin Ruff. If I had but a thousand a year, Gaffer Green! If I had but a thousand a year! What a man would I be, And what sights would I see, If I had but a thousand a year, Gaffer Green! If I had but a thou-sand a year!

Gaffer Green. The best wish you could have, take my word, Robin Ruff,
    Would scarce find you in bread or in beer;
      But be honest and true,
      And say what would you do,
    If you had but a thousand a year, Robin Ruff,
      If you had but a thousand a year.

Robin Ruff. I'd do, I scarcely know what, Gaffer Green,
    I'd go, faith! I hardly know where,
      I'd scatter the chink
      And leave others to think,
    If I had but a thousand a year, Gaffer Green,
      If I had but a thousand a year!

Gaffer Green. But when you are aged and grey, Robin Ruff,
    And the day of your death, it draws near,
      Say, what with your pains,
      Would you do with your gains,
    If you then had a thousand a year, Robin Ruff?
      If you then had a thousand a year?

Robin Ruff. I scarcely can tell, what you mean, Gaffer Green,
    For your questions are always so queer,
      But as other folks die,
      I suppose so must I—
Gaffer Green. What! and give up your thousand a year, Robin Ruff,
    And give up your thousand a year?

    There's a place that is better than this, Robin Ruff,
    And I hope in my heart you'll go there,
      Where the poor man's as great,
Robin Ruff.   What, though he hath no estate?
Gaffer Green. Yes, as if he'd a thousand a year, Robin Ruff,
Gaffer Green.
Robin Ruff. } Yes, as if he'd a thousand a year.

BRINGING IN THE SHEAVES. 293.

Matt. 13 : 39. GEORGE A. MINOR.

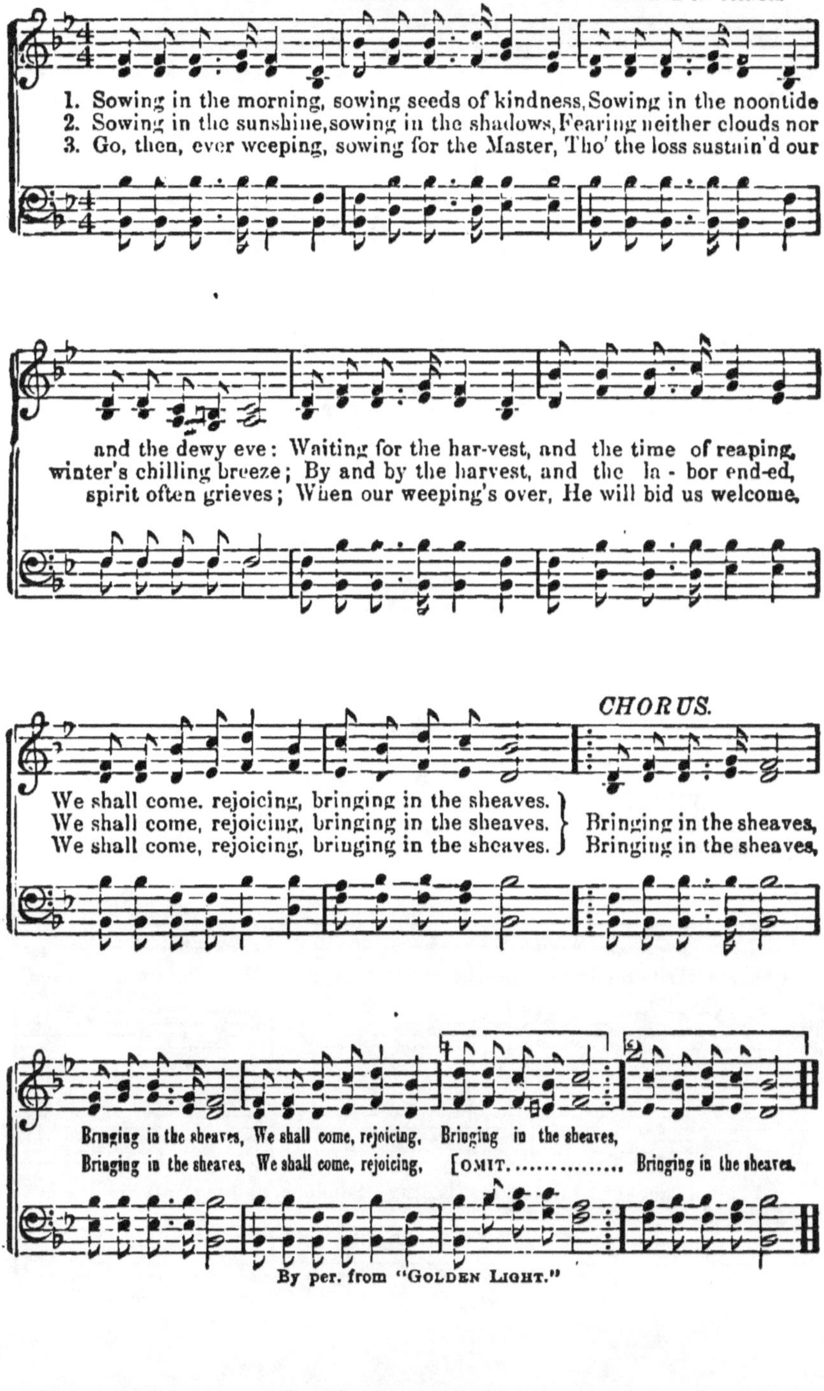

By per. from "GOLDEN LIGHT."

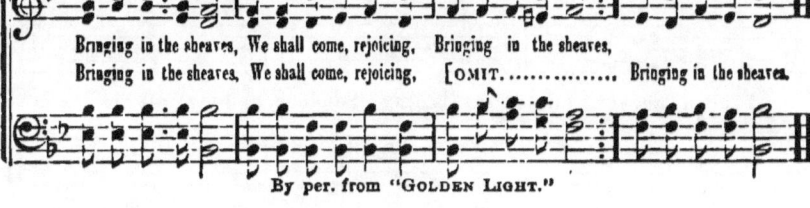

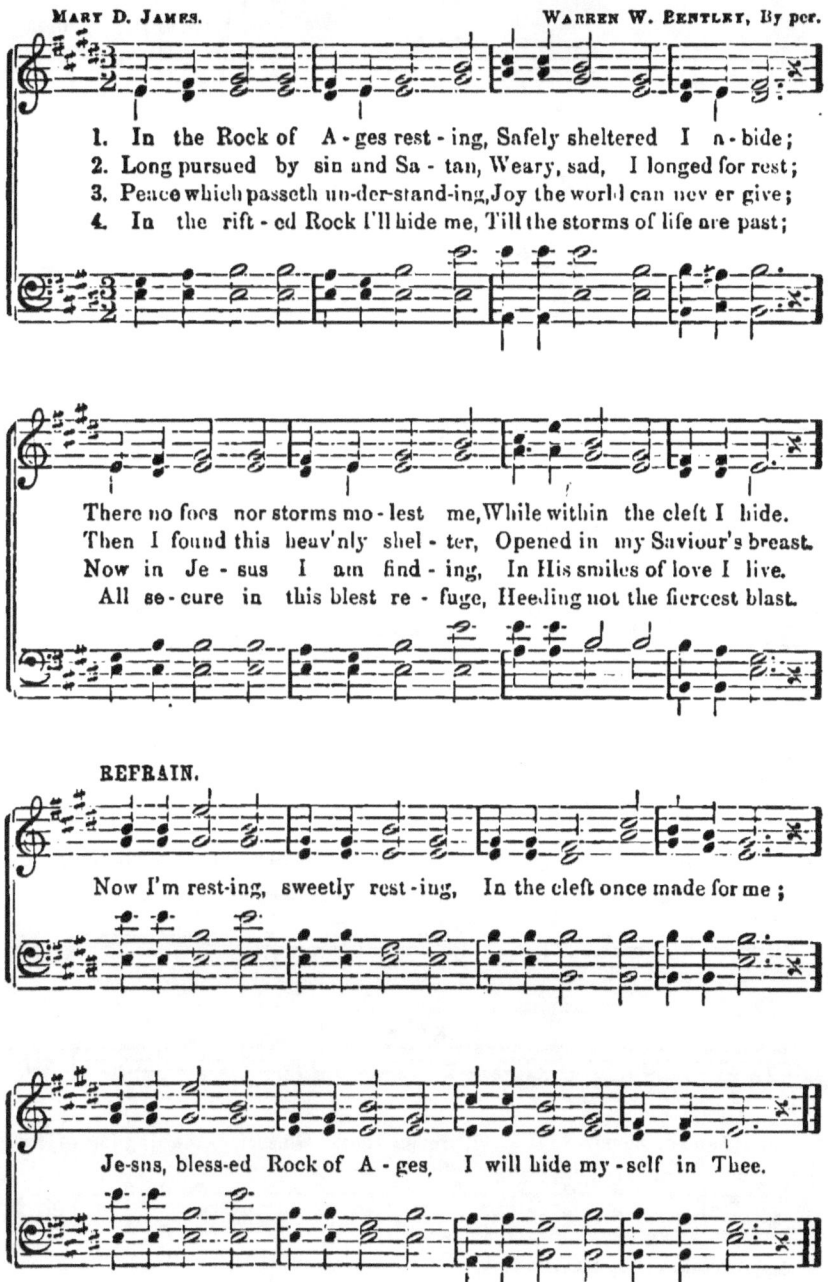

296. SEEK YE THE KINGDOM OF GOD.

(Matt. vi. 33.)

Words and Music by R. E. HUDSON.

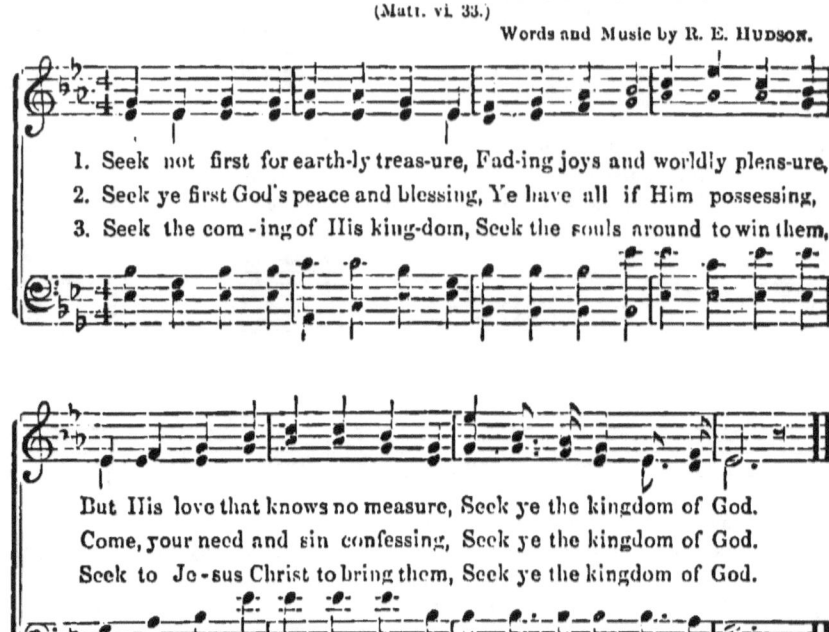

1. Seek not first for earth-ly treas-ure, Fad-ing joys and worldly pleas-ure,
But His love that knows no measure, Seek ye the kingdom of God.

2. Seek ye first God's peace and blessing, Ye have all if Him possessing,
Come, your need and sin confessing, Seek ye the kingdom of God.

3. Seek the com-ing of His king-dom, Seek the souls around to win them,
Seek to Je-sus Christ to bring them, Seek ye the kingdom of God.

CHORUS.

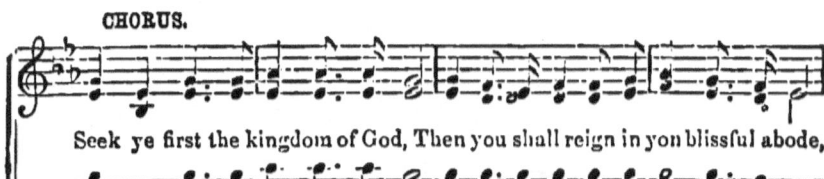

Seek ye first the kingdom of God, Then you shall reign in yon blissful abode,

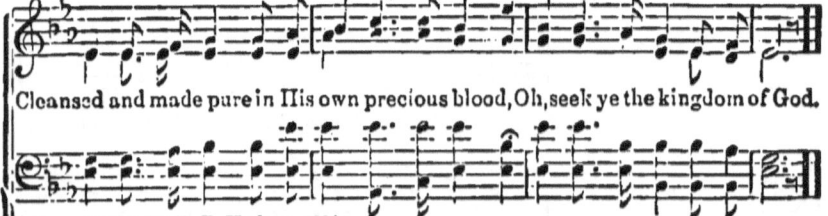

Cleansed and made pure in His own precious blood, Oh, seek ye the kingdom of God.

Copyrighted, by R. E. Hudson, 1884.

HE WILL GATHER THE WHEAT. 299.

Harriet B. M'Keever. Jno. R. Sweney.

1. When Jesus shall gath-er the na-tions Be-fore Him at
2. Shall we hear from the lips of the Sav-iour, The words "Faithful
3. Then let us be watch-ing and wait-ing, Our lamps burn-ing

last to ap-pear, Then, oh, how shall we stand in the judg-ment,
serv-ant, well done;" Or, trembling with fear and with an-guish,
stead-y and bright, When the Bridegroom shall call to the wed-ding,

CHORUS.

When summoned our sentence to hear? He will gath-er the wheat in His
Be banished a-way from His throne?
Our spir-its made ready for flight.

gar-ner, But the chaff will He scat-ter a-way; Then, oh,

how shall we stand in the judg-ment Of the great Re-sur-rec-tion Day?

From "The Garner." by per.

306. LILY OF THE VALLEY.

(As sung by Miss Belle McIlfried and Miss Fannie Emmel.)

Arranged by R. E. HUDSON.

1. I've found a friend in Jesus, He's everything to me, He's the fairest of ten thousand to my soul; The Lily of the Valley in Him alone I see, All I need to cleanse and make me fully whole, In sorrow He's my comfort, in trouble He's my stay, He tells me every care on Him to roll. He's the Lily of the

2. He all my griefs has taken, And all my sorrows borne. In temptation He's my strong and mighty tow'r; I've all for Him forsaken, I've all my idols torn From my heart, and now He keeps me by His pow'r; Tho' all the world forsake me, and Satan tempts me sore, Through Jesus I shall safely reach the goal. He's the Lily of the

3. He'll never, never leave me, Nor yet forsake me here, While I live by faith and do His blessed will; A wall of fire about me, I've nothing now to fear; With His manna He my hungry soul shall fill; Then sweeping up to glory to see His blessed face, Where rivers of delight shall ever flow. He's the Lily of the

Cho.—In sorrow He's my comfort, in trouble He's my stay; He tells me every care on Him to roll. He's the Lily of the

308. CHURCH OF GOD, AWAKE.

Mrs. E. J. Bugbee. T. C. O'Kane, by per.

1. Church of God, whose conquering banners Float along the glorious years, Gath'ring harvest rich and gold-en, Sowed in pov-er-ty and tears: Onward press, the cross is bend-ing Far to-ward the morning skies, Speedy dawn of light por-tend-ing;—Church of God, a-wake, a-rise!

2. In your cost-ly tem-ples pray-ing, "Let thy kingdom come," ye pray, Are but words of i-dle mean-ing, If with these ye turn a-way; Boundless wealth to you is giv-en, From His hand who owns it all, And His eye beholds in heav-en What ye ren-der back for all.

3. Grace and glo-ry He hath sent you, Cast your lines in pla-ces fair, Scat-ter blessing *now* He bids you, O'er His green earth everywhere; Till the millions in the twi-light Of the far-off O-rient land, In the gracious morning splendor Of the Gos-pel light shall stand.

CHORUS.

Church of God,...... awake! a-rise! Christ, your Head... and Master cries,
Church of God, a-wake! arise! Christ, your Head and Master, cries,

CHURCH OF GOD, AWAKE.—Concluded.

Send the Gos - pel's joy-ful sound, Unto-earth's re - mot - est bound.
Oh, send the Gos - pel's joy-ful sound,

WEIGHED IN THE BALANCE. 309.

Mrs. E. C. Ellsworth. By per. R. B. Mahaffey.

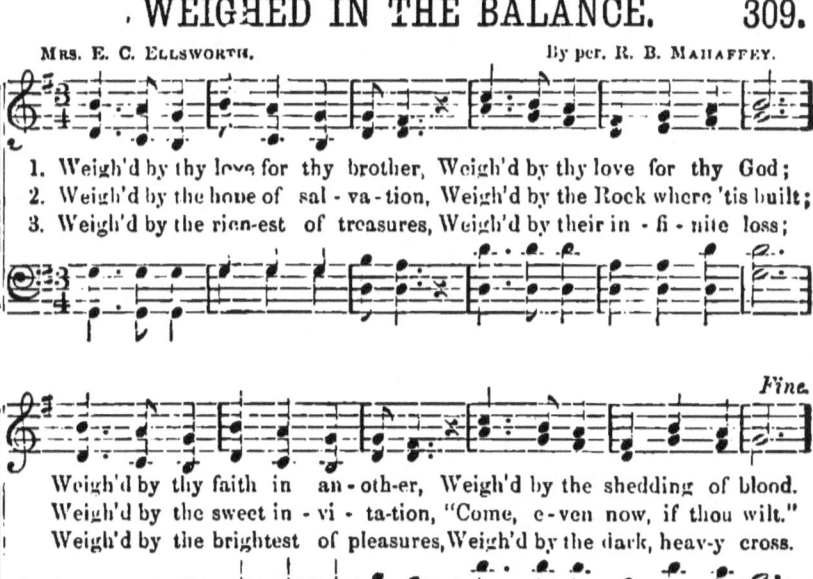

1. Weigh'd by thy love for thy brother, Weigh'd by thy love for thy God;
2. Weigh'd by the hope of sal - va - tion, Weigh'd by the Rock where 'tis built;
3. Weigh'd by the rich-est of treasures, Weigh'd by their in - fi - nite loss;

Fine.

Weigh'd by thy faith in an - oth - er, Weigh'd by the shedding of blood.
Weigh'd by the sweet in - vi - ta - tion, "Come, e - ven now, if thou wilt."
Weigh'd by the brightest of pleasures, Weigh'd by the dark, heav-y cross.

D.S. *Weigh'd, but thy soul has been trifling, Weigh'd, but found lighter than air.*

REFRAIN. *D.S.*

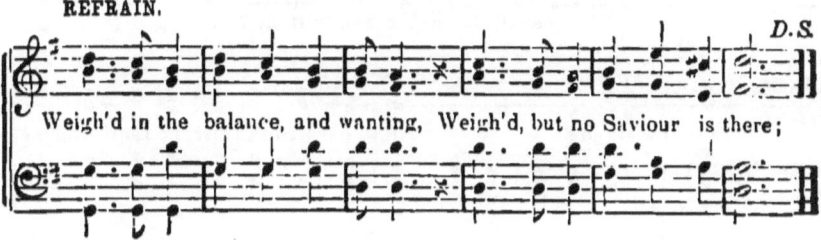

Weigh'd in the balance, and wanting, Weigh'd, but no Saviour is there;

WHO SHALL BE ABLE?—Concluded.

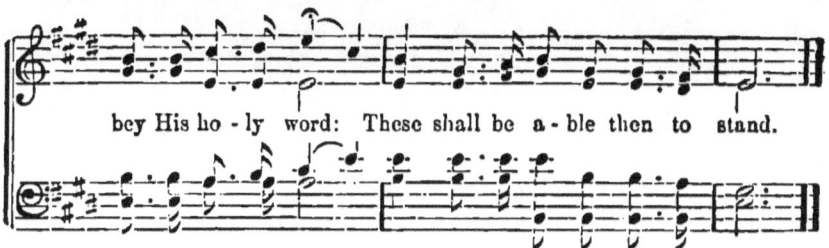

bey His ho-ly word: These shall be a-ble then to stand.

HE WOULD NOT GO AWAY. 311.

J. W. McABEE.

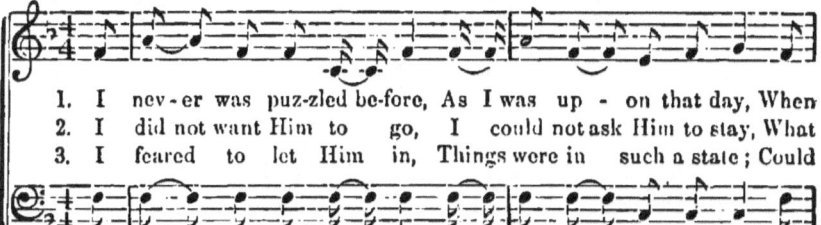

1. I nev-er was puz-zled be-fore, As I was up-on that day, When
2. I did not want Him to go, I could not ask Him to stay, What
3. I feared to let Him in, Things were in such a state ; Could

Cho.—Oh, come to the Saviour now, Where sin-ners are forgiven ; Oh,

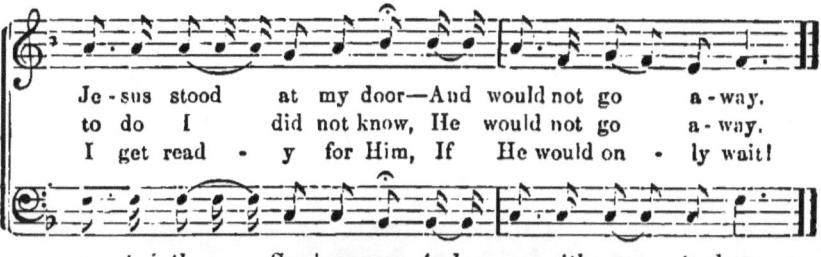

Je-sus stood at my door—And would not go a-way.
to do I did not know, He would not go a-way.
I get read-y for Him, If He would on-ly wait!

come to the Sav-iour now, And go with me to heaven.

4 I thought in time I might
   With some of my sins make way,
   Or hide them out of sight—
   But He would not go away.

5 Mine eyes with tears were dim,
   And all the night and day
   I could only think of Him,
   For He would not go away.

Copyrighted, 1885, by R. E. Hudson.

6 At last I ceased to weep,
   Then I forgot to pray,
   The door of my heart I could not keep,
   I asked Him in to stay.

Chorus after last verse.
He is my Saviour now,
   My sins are all forgiven ;
He is my Saviour now,
   I'm on my way to heaven.

PEACE DIVINE.—Concluded.

Copyrighted, 1885, by R. E. Hudson and I. N. McHose.

WELCOME TO GLORY. 313.

Words by Mrs. P. Palmer. Mrs. J. F. Knapp, by per.

1. O, when shall I sweep thro' the gates!
   The scenes of mortality o'er,
   What then for my spirit awaits?
   Will they sing on the glorified shore?

   CHORUS.
   Welcome home! welcome home!
   A welcome in glory for me;
   Welcome home! welcome home!
   A welcome for me!

2. When from Calvary's mount I rise,
   And pass through the portals above,
   Will shouts, Welcome home to the skies!
   Resound through the regions of love?

3. Yes! loved ones who knew me below,
   Who learned the new song with me here,
   In chorus will hail me, I know,
   And welcome me home with good cheer!

4. The beautiful gates will unfold,
   The home of the blood-washed I'll see;
   The city of saints I'll behold!
   For, O! there's a welcome for me!

5. A sinner made whiter than snow,
   I'll join in the mighty acclaim,
   And shout through the gates as I go,
   Salvation to God and the Lamb!

CALVARY.—Concluded.

Copyrighted, 1884, by R. E. HUDSON.

REDEEMED. 315.

Words and music by R. E. HUDSON.

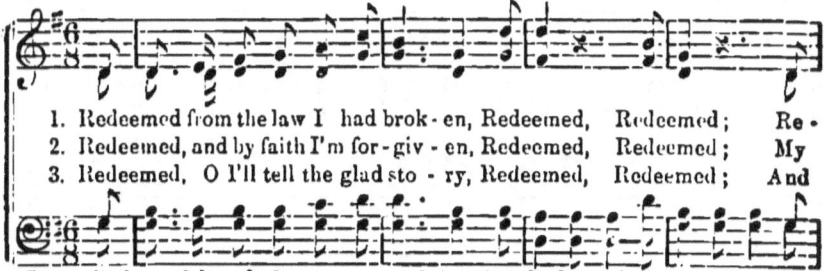

1. Redeemed from the law I had brok-en, Redeemed, Redeemed; Re-
2. Redeemed, and by faith I'm for-giv-en, Redeemed, Redeemed; My
3. Redeemed, O I'll tell the glad sto-ry, Redeemed, Redeemed; And

Cho.—Redeemed, how I love to pro-claim it! Redeemed, Redeemed; Re-

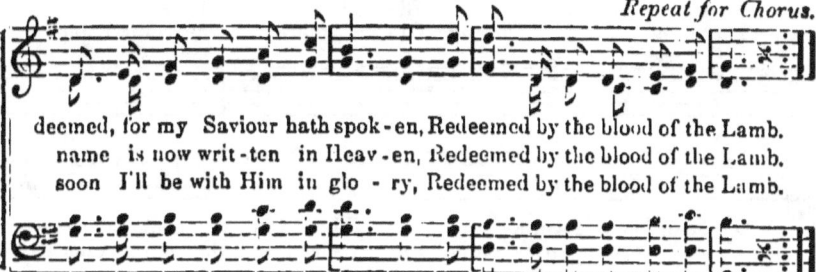

deemed, for my Saviour hath spok-en, Redeemed by the blood of the Lamb.
name is now writ-ten in Heav-en, Redeemed by the blood of the Lamb.
soon I'll be with Him in glo-ry, Redeemed by the blood of the Lamb.

deemed, how I love to pro-claim it! Redeemed by the blood of the Lamb.

Copyrighted, 1884, by R. E. HUDSON.

CLEANSING BALM.—Concluded.

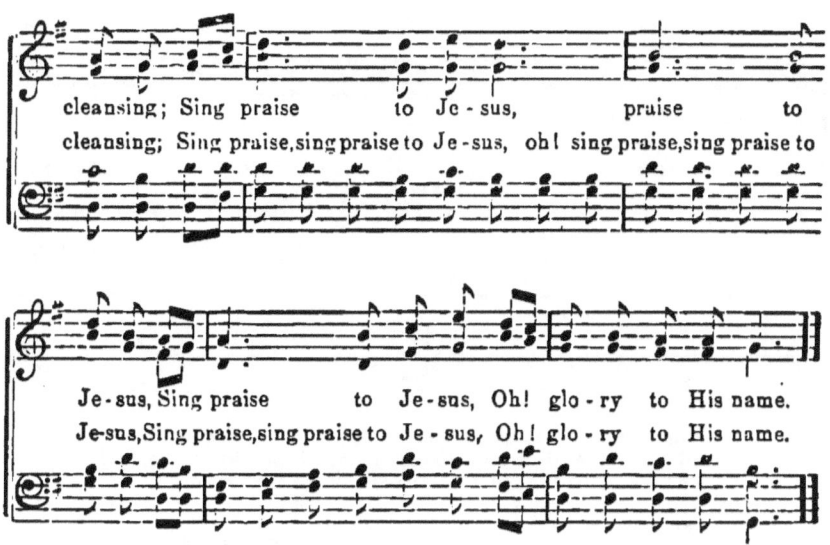

Copyrighted, 1884, By Kelso Carter.

STAY, SINNER, STAY. 317.

Arranged by R. E. H.

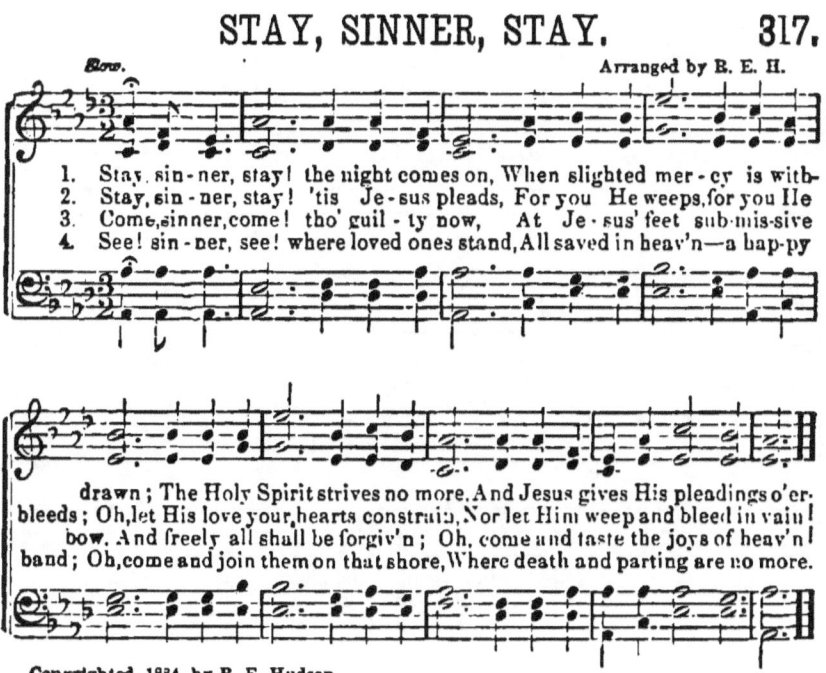

1. Stay, sin-ner, stay! the night comes on, When slighted mer-cy is withdrawn; The Holy Spirit strives no more, And Jesus gives His pleadings o'er.
2. Stay, sin-ner, stay! 'tis Je-sus pleads, For you He weeps, for you He bleeds; Oh, let His love your hearts constrain, Nor let Him weep and bleed in vain!
3. Come, sinner, come! tho' guil-ty now, At Je-sus' feet sub-mis-sive bow, And freely all shall be forgiv'n; Oh, come and taste the joys of heav'n!
4. See! sin-ner, see! where loved ones stand, All saved in heav'n—a hap-py band; Oh, come and join them on that shore, Where death and parting are no more.

Copyrighted, 1884, by R. E. Hudson.

320   JESUS, LOVER OF MY SOUL.

C. WESLEY.   R. E. HUDSON.

2. Thou, O Christ, art all I want:
 More than all in thee I find:
 Raise the fallen, cheer the faint,
 Heal the sick and lead the blind.
 Just and holy is thy name;
 I am all unrighteousness;
 False, and full of sin I am;
 Thou art full of truth and grace.

3. Plenteous grace with thee is found,—
 Grace to cover all my sin;
 Let the healing streams abound:
 Make and keep me pure within,
 Thou of life the fountain art;
 Freely let me take of thee:
 Spring thou up within my heart,
 Rise to all eternity.

322. I WILL GIVE YOU REST.

AMICUS. L. BALTZELL.

1. Come, wea-ry soul, sin-burdened and distressed, Je-sus now waits to give the promised rest; Hast-en, O wanderer, at His footstool bow;
2. See mer-cy's boundless wa-ters free-ly flow, To cleanse thy heart and ban-ish eve-ry woe; Par-don and peace and end-less life He'll give,
3. Haste, sin-ner, haste, while mercy may be found, Soon may be hushed the Gos-pel's joy-ous sound; Hear Je-sus say to eve-ry soul oppressed:
4. Je-sus, I come, O help my un-be-lief! Now I am trust-ing, give my soul re-lief! Wash me, O Sav-iour, in thy cleansing blood,

CHORUS. *Tenderly.*

On-ly be-lieve Him, He will save you now.
On-ly be-lieve Him, on-ly look and live. Come un-to me,
"Come un-to me, and I will give you rest."
Seal me thine own, O precious Lamb of God.

Rit. ad lib.

come un-to me, Come un-to me and I will give you rest.

Copyrighted, 1884, by R. E. HUDSON.

SAFETY.

Music by R. E. H. 325

2. Could my tears forever flow,
   Could my zeal no languor know,
   These for sin could not atone;
   Thou must save, and Thou alone:
   In my hand no price I bring;
   Simply to the cross I cling.

3. While I draw this fleeting breath,
   When my eyes shall close in death,
   When I rise to worlds unknown,
   And behold Thee on Thy throne,
   Rock of Ages, cleft for me,
   Let me hide myself in Thee.

Copyrighted, 1882, by R. E. HUDSON.

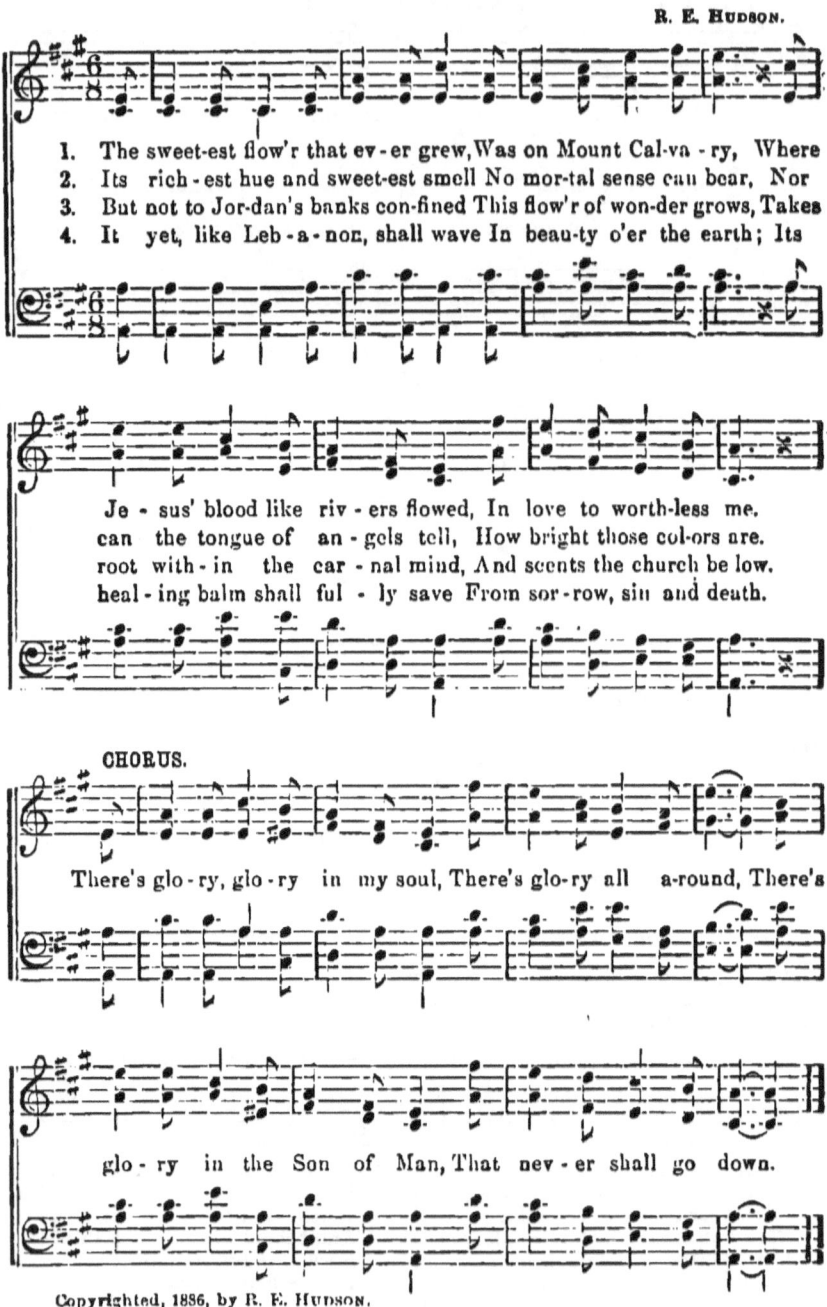

BLESSED JESUS, THOU ART MINE.—Concluded.

I am safe within the fold,
All my cares on thee are rolled,
I enjoy the sweetest rest,
For I'm leaning on thy breast;
Blessed Jesus, keep me white,
Keep me walking in the light.

3. Precious Jesus, day by day
Keep me in the holy way;
Keep my mind in perfect peace;
Every day my faith increase;
Blessed Jesus, keep me white,
Keep me walking in the light.

SATISFIED. 337.

Miss Clara Teare.   Psalms 36 : 8.   R. E. Hudson.

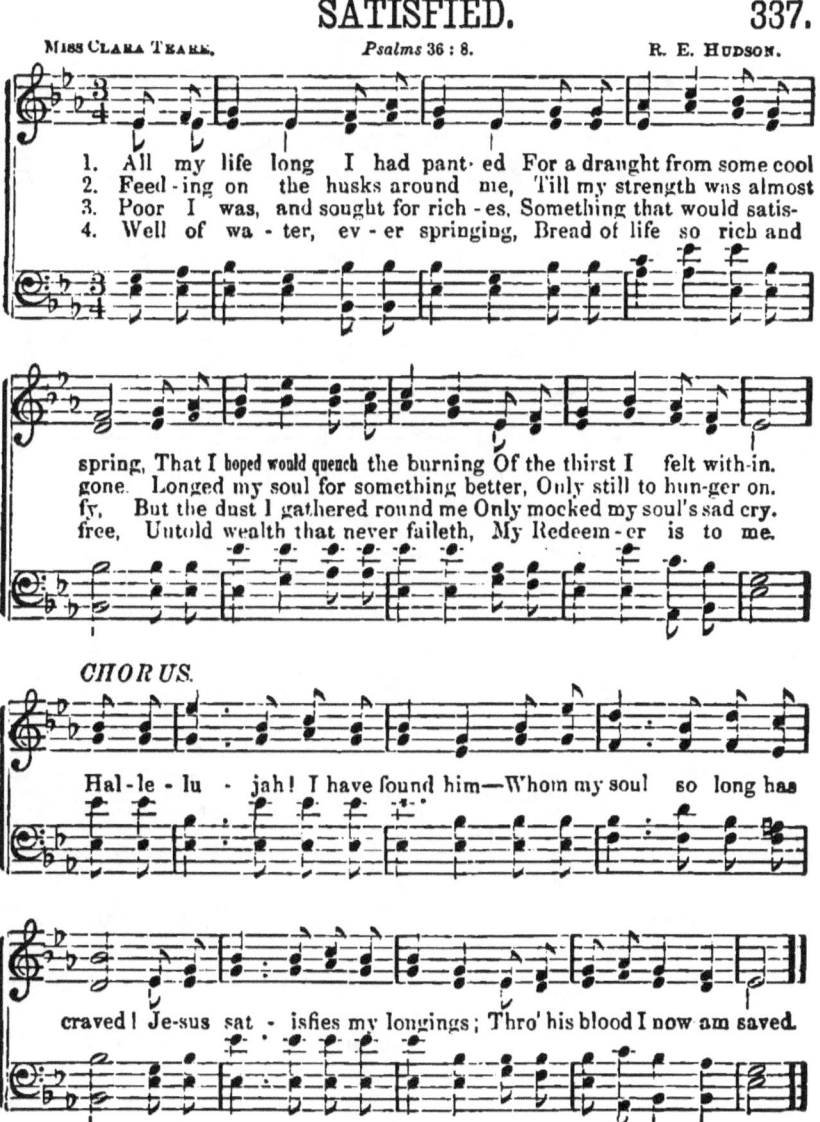

1. All my life long I had pant-ed For a draught from some cool spring, That I hoped would quench the burning Of the thirst I felt with-in.
2. Feed-ing on the husks around me, Till my strength was almost gone. Longed my soul for something better, Only still to hun-ger on.
3. Poor I was, and sought for rich-es, Something that would satis-fy, But the dust I gathered round me Only mocked my soul's sad cry.
4. Well of wa-ter, ev-er springing, Bread of life so rich and free, Untold wealth that never faileth, My Redeem-er is to me.

CHORUS.

Hal-le-lu-jah! I have found him—Whom my soul so long has craved! Je-sus sat-isfies my longings; Thro' his blood I now am saved.

3. Thou dying Lamb, ‖: thy precious blood.:‖
Thou dying Lamb, thy precious blood
Shall never lose its power,
Till all the ransomed ‖: Church of God.:‖
Till all the ransomed Church of God
Are saved, to sin no more.

4. E'er since by faith ‖: I saw the stream,:‖
E'er since by faith I saw the stream
Thy flowing wounds supply,
Redeeming love ‖: has been my theme,:‖
Redeeming love has been my theme,
And shall be till I die.

Copyrighted, 1881, by T. C. O'KANE.

343. RING, RING THE BELLS.

Words and Music by R. E. HUDSON.

1. Christmas bells are ring-ing, Mer-ry bells, joy-ful bells,
2. Christmas bells are ring-ing, Peace on earth, good news bring,
3. Christmas bells are ring-ing, Heav'n-ly bells, earth-ly bells,

Hap-py news are bring-ing, Je-sus is our King!
Chil-dren now are sing-ing, Je-sus is our King!
Love and peace are bring-ing, Je-sus is our King!

CHORUS.
Ring, ring the bells, Ring, ring, Ring, ring the bells, Glad good news to earth they bring;
Ring, ring the bells, Ring, ring, Ring, ring the bells, Je-sus is our King!

Copyrighted, 1884, by R. E. Hudson.

344. TUNE—THE CROSS. E.

1 The cross! the cross! the blood-stained cross!
The hallowed cross I see!
Reminding me of precious blood
That once was shed for me.

Cho.—Oh, the blood! the precious blood!
That Jesus shed for me,
Upon the cross, in crimson flood,
Just now by faith I see.

2 The cross! the cross! the heavy cross!
My Saviour bore for me,
Which bowed Him to the earth with grief
On sad Mount Calvary.

3 How light! how light! this precious cross,
Presented to my view;
And while, with care, I take it up,
Behold the crown my due.

THIS LOVE SO FREE. 345.

M. M. J.   MARK M JONES.

1. How tenderly Jesus loves us, With love so pure and free,
2. His love so freely given, Was purchas'd with the blood,
3. Beneath that purple fountain, That flows from Jesus' side,
4. And now the Savior begs us, 'This precious blood receive,

Down from his throne above us, It comes to you and me.
That from his dear side riven, Pours forth a saving flood.
Down o-ver Calvary's mountain, We safely may abide.
And all that it will cost us, Is simply to believe.

CHORUS.
Oh, who can conceive it, Oh, who can believe it,
Oh, who will receive it, This love so free?...

TUNE—HE LEADETH ME. D.   346.

1 He leadeth me! Oh! blessed thought,
Oh, words with heav'nly comfort fraught;
Whate'er I do, where'er I be,
Still 'tis God's hand that leadeth me.

CHORUS.
He leadeth me, He leadeth me;
By His own hand He leadeth me;
His faithful follower I would be,
For by His hand He leadeth me.

2 Sometimes 'mid scenes of deepest gloom,
Sometimes where Eded's bowers bloom;
By waters still o'er troubled sea—
Still 'tis His hand that leadeth me.

3 Lord, I would clasp thy hand in mine,
Nor ever murmur or repine,—
Content, whatever lot I see,
Since 'tis my God that leadeth me.

347. JESUS SAVES ME ALL THE TIME.

Jas. Nicholson.   J. A. Duncan.

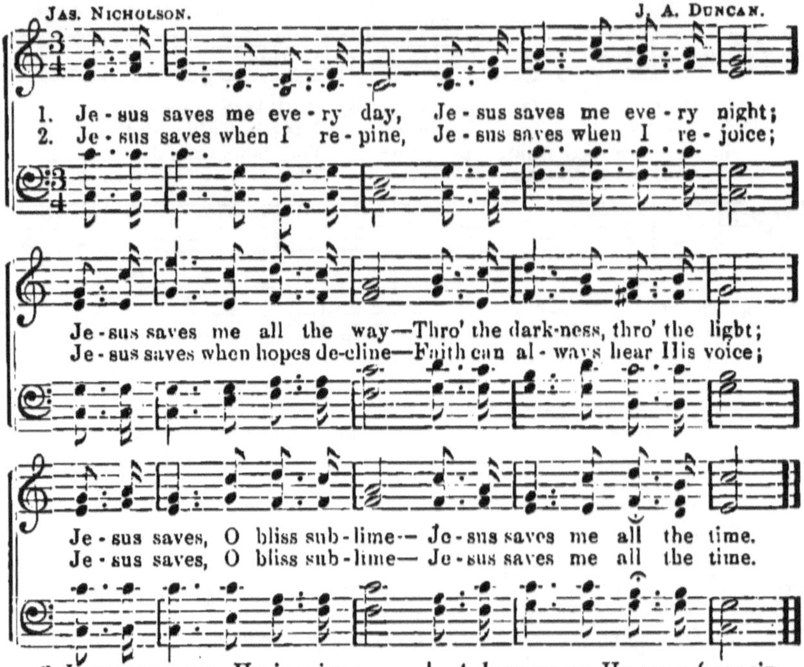

1. Je-sus saves me eve-ry day, Je-sus saves me eve-ry night;
2. Je-sus saves when I re-pine, Je-sus saves when I re-joice;

Je-sus saves me all the way—Thro' the dark-ness, thro' the light;
Je-sus saves when hopes de-cline—Faith can al-ways hear His voice;

Je-sus saves, O bliss sub-lime— Je-sus saves me all the time.
Je-sus saves, O bliss sub-lime— Je-sus saves me all the time.

3 Jesus saves me, He is mine;
   Jesus saves me, I am His;
   Jesus saves while I recline—
   On His precious promises.

4 Jesus saves, He saves from sin,
   Jesus saves, I feel Him nigh;
   Jesus saves, He dwells within,
   Gladly do I testify.

348. I AM JESUS' LITTLE LAMB.

Words and Music by R. E. Hudson.

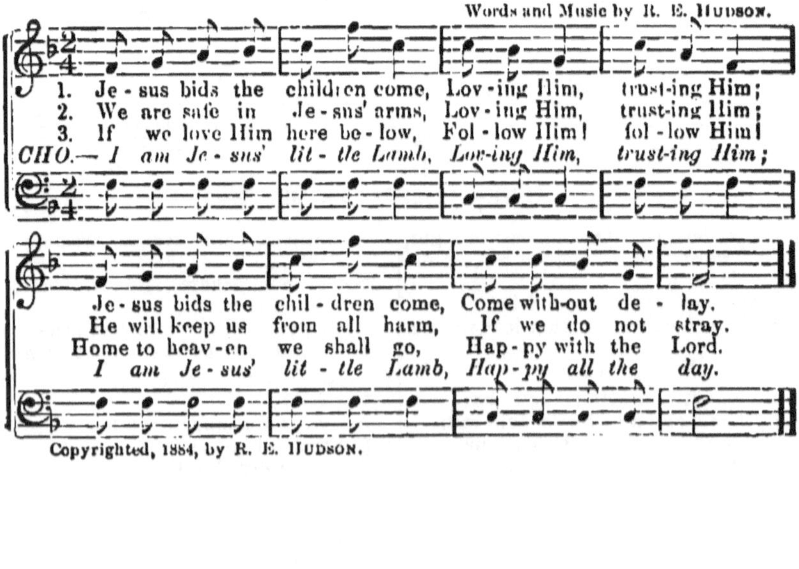

1. Je-sus bids the children come, Lov-ing Him, trust-ing Him;
2. We are safe in Je-sus' arms, Lov-ing Him, trust-ing Him;
3. If we love Him here be-low, Fol-low Him! fol-low Him!
CHO.— I am Je-sus' lit-tle Lamb, Lov-ing Him, trust-ing Him;

Je-sus bids the chil-dren come, Come with-out de-lay.
He will keep us from all harm, If we do not stray.
Home to heav-en we shall go, Hap-py with the Lord.
I am Je-sus' lit-tle Lamb, Hap-py all the day.

Copyrighted, 1884, by R. E. Hudson.

HE KNOWS. 349.

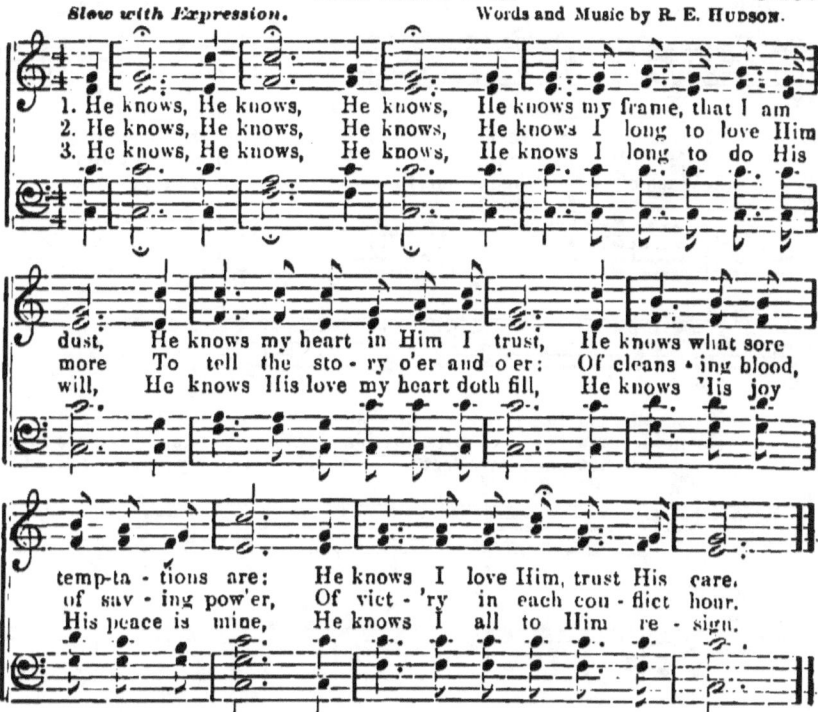

Slow with Expression. Words and Music by R. E. Hudson.

1. He knows, He knows, He knows, He knows my frame, that I am dust, He knows my heart in Him I trust, He knows what sore tempta-tions are: He knows I love Him, trust His care.
2. He knows, He knows, He knows, He knows I long to love Him more To tell the sto-ry o'er and o'er: Of cleans-ing blood, of sav-ing pow'er, Of vict-'ry in each con-flict hour.
3. He knows, He knows, He knows, He knows I long to do His will, He knows His love my heart doth fill, He knows 'tis joy His peace is mine, He knows I all to Him re-sign.

350. HOW FIRM A FOUNDATION. F.

1 How firm a foundation,
  Ye saints of the Lord,
Is laid for your faith
  In His excellent Word!
What more can He say
  Than to you he hath said,
You who unto Jesus
  For refuge have fled!

2 Fear not, I am with thee;
  Oh, be not dismayed;
I, I am thy God, and
  Will still give thee aid;
I'll strengthen thee, help thee,
  And cause thee to stand,
Upheld by my righteous,
  Omnipotent hand.

3 When through the deep waters
  I call thee to go,
The rivers of woe shall
  Not thee overflow;
For I will be with thee,
  Thy troubles to bless,
And sanctify to thee
  Thy deepest distress.

351. MUSIC NO. 21.

1 O mourner in Zion,
  How blessed art thou,
For Jesus is waiting
  To comfort thee now.
Fear not to rely on
  The word of thy God,
Step out on the promise,
  And trust in the blood.

2 O ye who are hungry
  And thirsty, rejoice,
For ye shall be filled,
  Oh, hear His sweet voice!
Inviting you now
  To the banquet of God,
Step out on the promise,
  And trust in the blood.

3 The promise don't save,
  Though each promise be true,
'Tis the blood when applied
  That cleanseth us through,
It cleanseth me now,
  Oh, glory to God!
I am out on the promise,
  I trust in the blood.

352. I WILL TRUST.

C. WESLEY. By per. T. C. O'KANE.

1. For-ev-er here my rest shall be, Close to thy bleed-ing side;
2. My dy-ing Sav-iour and my God, Fountain for guilt and sin,
3. Wash me, and make me thus thine own: Wash me, and mine thou art;

This all my hope and all my plea, For me the Sav-iour died.
Sprin-kle me ev - er with thy blood, And cleanse, and keep me clean.
Wash me, but not my feet a - lone, My hands, my head, my heart.

CHORUS.

I will trust, I will trust, I will trust in the blood of the Lamb; I will trust, I will trust, I will trust in the blood of the Lamb.

353. I WILL GUIDE THEE.

1 Precious promise God hath given
   To the weary passer by,
On the way from earth to heaven,
   "I will guide thee with Mine eye."
REF—I will guide thee, I will guide thee,
   I will guide thee with Mine eye;
On the way from earth to heaven
   I will guide thee with Mine eye.

When temptations almost win thee,
   And thy trusted watchers fly;
Let this promise ring within thee,
   "I will guide thee with Mine eye."
When the shades of life are falling,
   And the hour has come to die;
Hear thy trusty pilot calling,
   "I will guide thee with Mine eye."

AT THE FOUNTAIN. 354.

From "Revivalist."

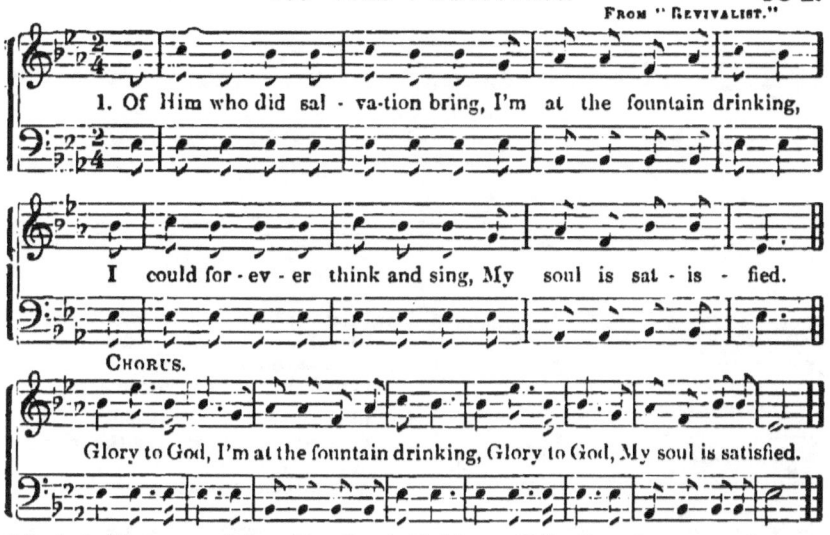

1. Of Him who did sal-va-tion bring, I'm at the fountain drinking, I could for-ev-er think and sing, My soul is sat-is-fied.

CHORUS.

Glory to God, I'm at the fountain drinking, Glory to God, My soul is satisfied.

2. Lo! glad I come; and thou, blest Lamb,
Shalt take me to thee, as I am:
Nothing but sin have I to give,—
Nothing but love shall I receive.

3. Then will I tell to sinners round,
What a dear Savior I have found;
I'll point to thy redeeming blood,
And say,—Behold the way to God.

ENOUGH FOR ME. 355.

E. A. H. E. A. H. By Per

1. O love surpassing knowledge! O grace so full and free! I know that Jesus saves me, And know that Je-sus saves me, And that's enough for me! And that's enough for me! And that's enough for me! I that's enough for me!

2. O wonderful salvation!
From sin he makes me free!
I feel the sweet assurance,
And that's enough for me!

3. O blood of Christ so precious,
Poured out on Calvary!
I feel its cleansing power,
And that's enough for me!

Copyrighted, 1852, by R. E. HUDSON.

356. WHY DON'T YOU COME TO JESUS.

C. R. Dunbar, by per.

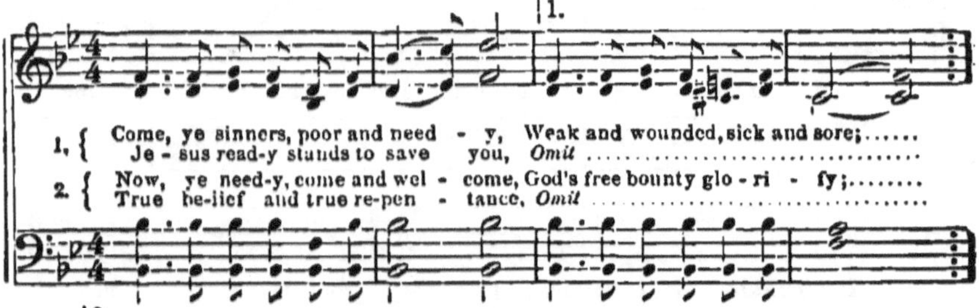

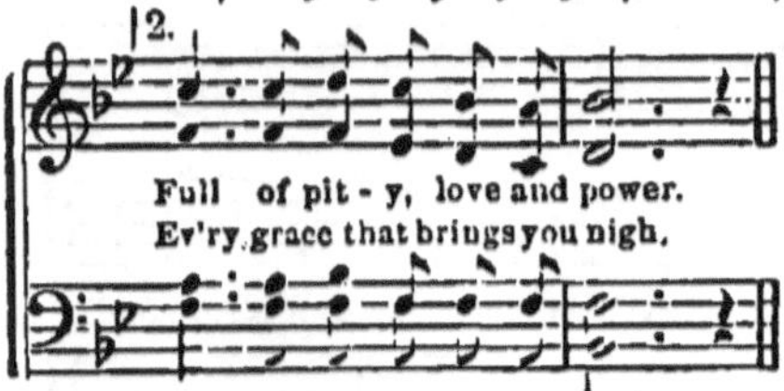

1. Come, ye sinners, poor and need-y, Weak and wounded, sick and sore;......
Je-sus read-y stands to save you, Omit ....
Full of pit-y, love and power.

2. Now, ye need-y, come and wel-come, God's free bounty glo-ri-fy;........
True be-lief and true re-pen-tance, Omit ....
Ev'ry grace that brings you nigh.

3 Let not conscience make you linger;
Nor of fitness fondly dream;
All the fitness he requireth
Is to feel your need of him!

4 Come ye weary, heavy-laden,
Bruised and mangled by the fall;
If you tarry 'till you're better,
You will never come at all;

CHORUS.

Why don't you come to Je-sus? He's wait-ing to receive you, Why don't you come to Je-sus and be saved?... saved?

357. HAVE YOU BEEN TO JESUS?   L.

1 Have you been to Jesus
For the cleansing power?
Are you washed
In the blood of the Lamb?
Are you fully trusting
In His grace this hour?
Are you washed
In the blood of the Lamb?

CHO.—Are you washed in the blood?
In the soul-cleansing blood
Of the Lamb?
Are your garments spotless?
Are they white as snow?
Are you washed
In the blood of the Lamb?

2 Are you walking daily
By the Saviour's side?
Are you washed
In the blood of the Lamb?
Do you rest each moment
In the Crucified?
Are you washed
In the blood of the Lamb?

3 When the Bridegroom cometh
Will your robes be white?
Pure and white,
In the blood of the Lamb?
Will your soul be ready,
For the mansions bright,
And be washed
In the blood of the Lamb?

GEMS OF GOSPEL SONG.

I WILL FOLLOW THEE. 358.

JAS. L. ELGINBURG.

1. I will follow thee, my Saviour, Wheresoe'er my lot may be;
2. Tho' the road be rough and thorny, Trackless as the foaming sea,

Where thou go-est I will fol-low, Yes, my Lord, I'll follow thee.
Thou hast trod this way before me, And I glad-ly follow thee.

CHORUS.

I will follow thee, my Saviour, Thou didst shed thy blood for me;
And tho' all men should forsake thee, By thy grace I'll follow thee.

3 Though 'tis lone, and dark, and dreary,
   Cheerless though my path may be,
   If thy voice I hear before me,
   Fearlessly I'll follow thee.

5 Tho' thou lead'st me thro' affliction,
   Poor, forsaken, though I be,
   Thou wast destitute, afflicted,
   And I only follow thee.

359. MY SAVIOUR KNOWS.

Mrs. E. W. Chapman.   Ps. 31:15.   J. H. Tenney.

1. The hour of my departure I may not know, But Christ in love hath taught me To watch while here below, My lamp to keep bright burning With oil divine, That at the Lord's appearing My soul with grace may shine.
2. The hour of my departure I'll keep in view, And strive, while here I linger, Some precious work to do, Some service for the Master, Or cross to bear, That I a crown unfading, And robe of white may wear.
3. The hour of my departure May soon be here; To me the thought is joyful, And yonder light is clear; I see the sunlit mountains Where I shall stand, I hear the songs enchanting Of yon celestial band.

REFRAIN.

The hour of my departure My Saviour knows, And, in his love confiding, I dwell in sweet repose.

3. Will you come, will you come, you have
    nothing to pay;
   Jesus, who loves you best.
   By his death on the Cross purchased life
    for your soul,
   Jesus will give you rest.

4. Will you come, will you come? how he
    pleads with you now!
   Fly to his loving breast;
   And whatever your sin or your sorrow
    may be,
   Jesus will give you rest.

371. THE OLD MOUNTAIN PINES.

Andrew Sherwood.   C. F. Dartt.
Solo.

1. When the night gath-ers cold, On the moor and the wold,
2. And I list to the brook, In the green, sha-dy nook,
3. But there's one sim-ple song, Which has lived all a-long,
4. Oh, my mem-o-ry twines Round the beau-ti-ful pines,
5. And long, long may it stand, An em-blem so grand,

Then my thoughts thro' the twilight will roam, Till in fan-cy I stand,
Mak-ing mu-sic so soft-ly and low; And the song of the bird,
For it fell in such smooth, flowing lines; 'Tis the song of the breeze
Wav-ing green in the glory of Spring; Standing high and a-lone,
Of the home to life's wanderer given, Which the weary soul finds,

In my dear native land, 'Neath the pines by my beauti-ful home.
Which my in-fan-cy heard, In that beau-ti-ful time, long a-go.
Com-ing up from the seas, In the boughs of the old mountain pines.
On the mountain's high throne, Where the winds in the long Summer sing.
'Mid the beau-ti-ful pines, On the gold-en sa-vannas of heaven.

CHORUS.

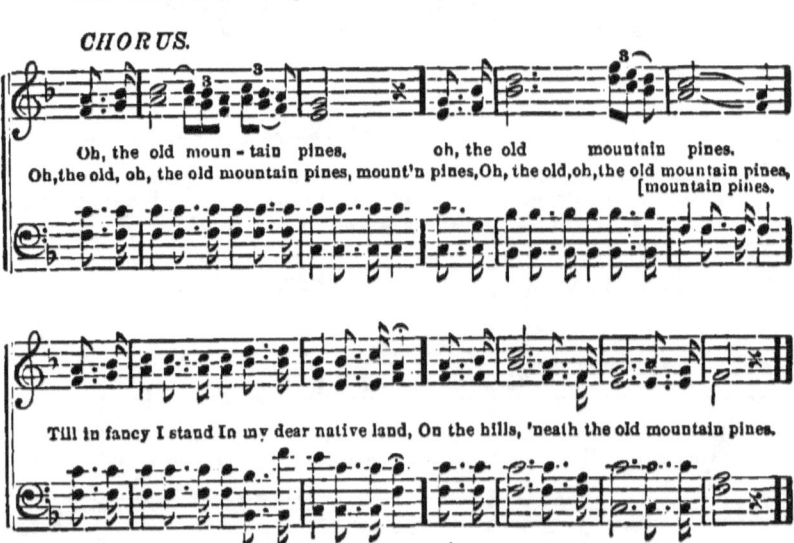

Oh, the old moun-tain pines, oh, the old mountain pines.
Oh, the old, oh, the old mountain pines, mount'n pines, Oh, the old, oh, the old mountain pines,
[mountain pines,

Till in fancy I stand In my dear native land, On the hills, 'neath the old mountain pines.

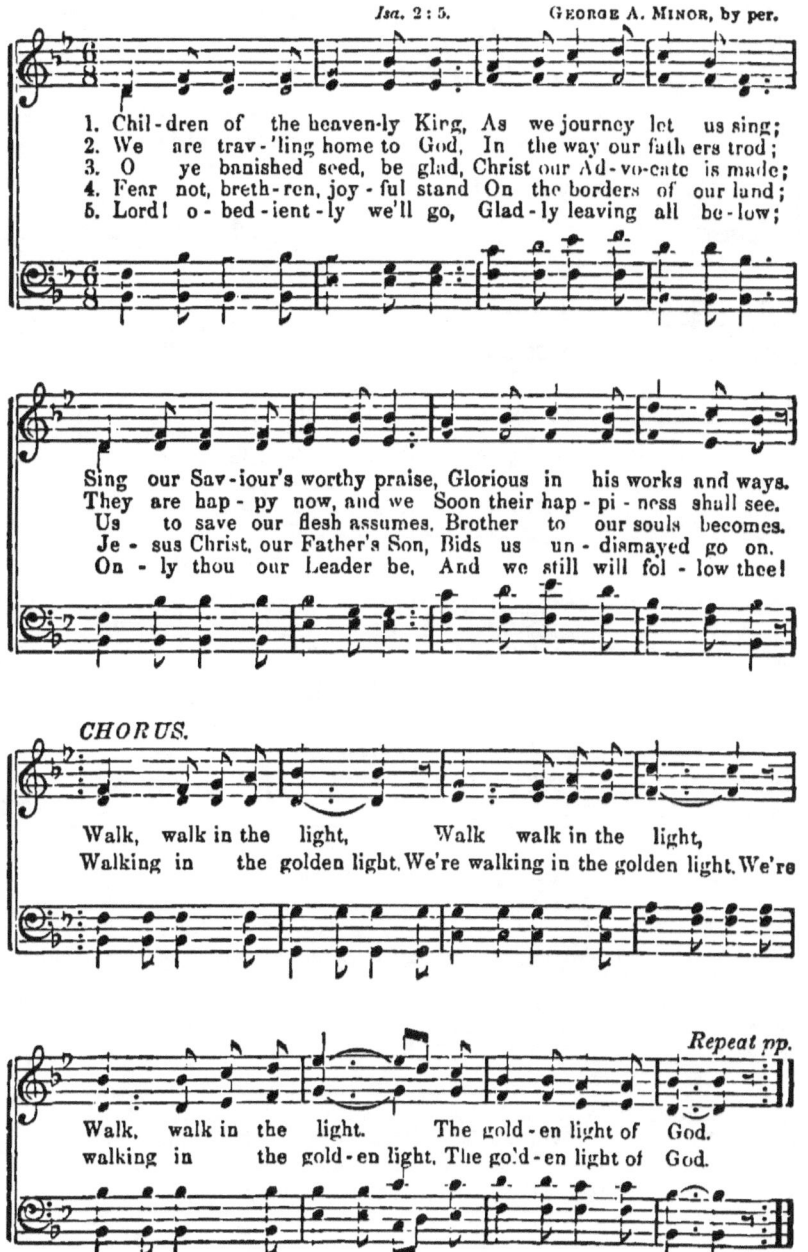

379. GATES OF THE BEAUTIFUL.

Rev. 21: 12.

ARTHUR W. FRENCH. J. H. TENNEY, by per.

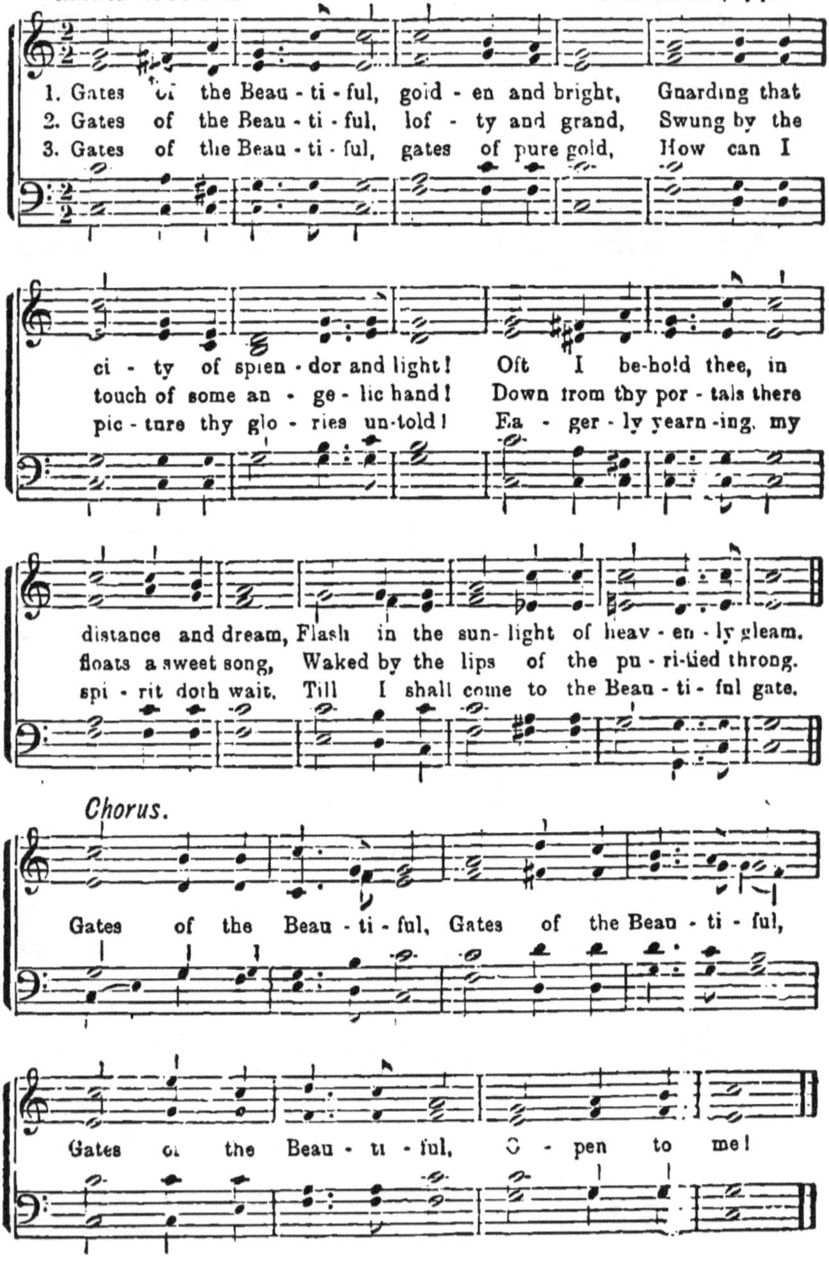

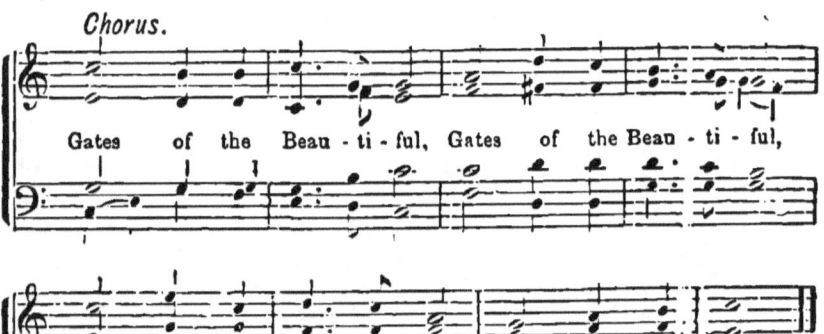

HOMEWARD BOUND.—Concluded.

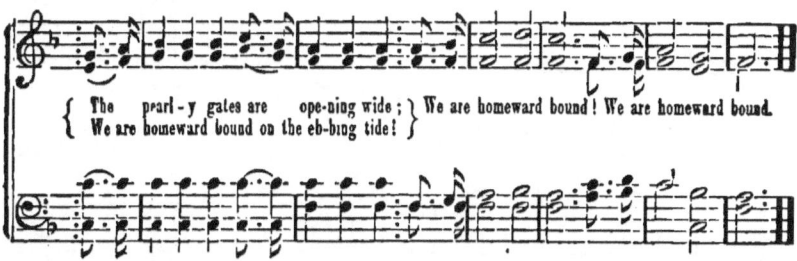

{ The pearl-y gates are ope-ning wide; } We are homeward bound! We are homeward bound.
{ We are homeward bound on the eb-bing tide! }

4. We float away from the care and strife,
From the din and bustle and toil of life,
Where temptation and sin shall be known no
And woe and pain are forever o'er— [more,
To the Eden-land, to the heavenly ground,
To the land of love we are homeward bound.

5. It soothes my heart like a blessed Psalm,
And bids its troubled waves be calm,
And its echo a far sweeter music tells
Than vesper chimes, or the Sabbath bells;
Floating thro' my life with a joy profound,
Is the blessed truth, we are homeward bound.

WHAT SHALL IT PROFIT ME THEN? 382

Mark 8: 36.

R. E. H.   R. E. HUDSON. *Fine.*

1. What shall it pro-fit me by and by? What shall it profit me then,
2. What shall it pro-fit me by and by? What shall it profit me then,
3. Naught will it pro-fit me by and by! Naught will it profit me then!
4. What shall it pro-fit me by and by? What shall it profit me then,

D. C. Trusting not him who for sinners was slain, What shall it profit me then?
Car - ing not, seeking not Jesus to know, What shall it profit me then?
Ev - er and ever its torment to know, Naught will it profit me then!
Love him, and serve him, and trust him alway, What shall it profit me then?

D. C.

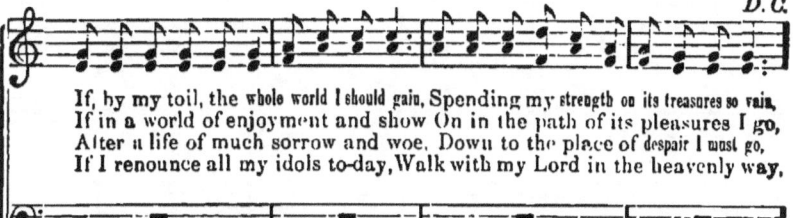

If, by my toil, the whole world I should gain, Spending my strength on its treasures so vain,
If in a world of enjoyment and show On in the path of its pleasures I go,
After a life of much sorrow and woe, Down to the place of despair I must go,
If I renounce all my idols to-day, Walk with my Lord in the heavenly way,

5. Much will it profit me by and by!
Much will it profit me then!
I shall be robed in a garment of white,
Dwell in the mansions of glory and light,
Gaze on the face of my Saviour so bright,
Much will it profit me then!

6. Yes, it will profit me by and by!
Yes, it will profit me then,
If from the right path my feet shall not stray,
If I but follow the Saviour alway,
Then when we meet in the great judgment
Oh, it will profit me then! [day,

THIS IS WHY I LOVE MY JESUS. 384.

Rev. Elisha A. Hoffman.

2. Would you know why I love Jesus?
   Why he is so dear to me?
   'Tis because the blood of Jesus
   Fully saves and cleanses me.

3. Would you know why I love Jesus?
   Why he is so dear to me?
   'Tis because, amid temptation,
   He supports and strengthens me.

4. Would you know why I love Jesus?
   Why he is so dear to me?
   'Tis because in every conflict
   Jesus gives me victory.

5. Would you know why I love Jesus?
   Why he is so dear to me?
   'Tis because, my friend and Savior
   He will ever, ever be.

I AM THE LIGHT. 388.

Theo. Hyatt. — John 8:12 — Jno. R. Sweney, by per.
Moderato.

1. My path is dark, Lord, very dark, No ray of light illumes my way;
A sweet voice whispers, Sad one, hark! [OMIT 2d time........]
Oh, hear the blest Redeemer say:

CHORUS.
I am the light, I am the light, yes, I am the light,
I am the light, I am the light, yes, I am the light,
Oh, walk in the light, oh, walk in the light, oh, walk in the light,
Then visions of bliss will break on thy sight, Break, break, break on thy sight;
Break, will break, will break, will
And the path I shall lead will ever be bright, Ever, yes, ever be bright!

2. I'm burdened, Lord, and sore opprest,
I faint beneath the heavy load;
But Jesus says, In Me find rest;
For all along the weary road,
I am the light, etc.

3. I'm vile, Lord, very very vile,
And sin assails with mighty power;
A whisper comes, a heavenly smile,
I'll cleanse thy heart this very hour.

4. I come, dear Lord, with every cloud,—
My burdens all to thee I bring,
And cast my sins, with praises loud,
On him whose wondrous grace I sing.

*Thou art the light! thou art the light!
Forever, dear Jesus, I'll walk in this light;
Lo, visions of bliss now break on my sight,—
It is glory, all glory, my pathway is bright,
Ever, yes, ever is bright!*

389. HEAR JESUS KNOCKING.

Mrs E. C. Ellsworth.   *Rev. 3 : 20.*   J. H. Tenney.

1. Hear Jesus knocking at the door of thy heart! Hasten! lest in weariness thy
2. Hear Jesus knocking, for he now comes to thee, He whose love is boundless, and whose
3. Hear Jesus knocking! ah! he turns, turns away! Sinner, wilt thou let him leave thee,

guest should depart! Long has he waited, and in love waits to-day,
grace makes us free; All things are ready; if thy heart thou wilt give,
or bid him stay? Soul, thou art starving, wilt thou still, still refuse?

CHORUS.

Ea-ger for thy coming, sinner, wilt thou delay? }
Je-sus then shall enter in, and thy soul shall live. } Oh! then receive him!
Hasten, thou art dying! sinner, death wilt thou choose? }

Christ shall be thine! Never didst thou en-ter-tain a guest so divine

Ne'er one so royal at thy door called for thee; Hasten to admit him, and thy Saviour he'll be

SALVATION ECHOES.
EXHORTATION. 390.

1. O! for a heart to praise my God, A heart from sin set free; A heart that always feels thy blood, So freely spilt for me.

2 A heart resign'd, submissive, meek,
My great Redeemer's throne;
Where only Christ is heard to speak,
Where Jesus reigns alone.

3 O for a lowly, contrite heart,
Believing, true, and clean;
Which neither life nor death can part,
From Him that dwells within.

4 A heart in every thought renewed,
And full of love divine;
Perfect, and right, and pure, and good,
A copy, Lord, of thine.

5 Thy nature, gracious Lord, impart;
Come quickly from above;
Write thy new name upon my heart,
Thy new, best name of Love.

391.

1 O for a thousand tongues, to sing
My great Redeemer's praise;
The glories of my God and King,
The triumphs of his grace.

2 My gracious Master, and my God,
Assist me to proclaim—
To spread, thro' all the earth abroad,
The honors of thy name.

3 Jesus! the Name that charms our fears,
That bids our sorrows cease;
'Tis music in the sinners ears,
'Tis life, and health, and peace.

4 He breaks the pow'r of cancel'd sin,
He sets the pris'ner free:
His blood can make the foulest clean;
His blood availed for me.

Copyrighted, 1882, by R. E. HUDSON.

3 I'm leaning on his loving breast
  Along life's weary way;
 My path, illumined by his smiles,
  Grows brighter every day
 No foes, no woes my heart can fear,
 With my almighty friend so near

4 I know his sheltering wings of love
  Are always o'er me spread,
 And tho' the storms may fiercely **rage**,
  All calm and free from dread,
 My peaceful spirit ever sings
 "I'll trust the covert of thy **wings**."

Copyrighted, 1882, by R. E. HUDSON.

396. NO ROOM IN HEAVEN.

W. O. CUSHING. I. BALTZELL, by per.

1. How sad it would be, if when thou dost call, All hopeless and unfor-given, The an-gel that stands at the beau-ti-ful gate, Should answer: No room in heaven!
2. How sad it would be, the harvest all past, The bright summer days all o-ver, To know that the reapers had gathered the grain, And left thee alone for-ev-er!
3. Oh! haste thee and fly, while mercy is near; Remember the love that he gave you; The love that hath sought thee is seeking thee still, And Jesus now waits to save you.

REFRAIN.

Sad, sad, sad would it be! No room in heav-en for thee! No room, no room, No room in heaven for thee!

Cho. for last verse—Room, room, still there is room, Oh! come while yet there is room; Still room, still room, Oh! come while yet there is room.

Slow and soft.

No room, no room, No room in heaven for thee! room; Still room, still room, Oh! come while yet there is room.

3. Lost but found! I now can sing
Vict'ry through my Savior King,
‖: Vict'ry ev'ry day and hour ; :‖
Vict'ry still will be my song
When I join the ransom'd throng,
‖: Vict'ry o'er the tempter's power. :‖

4. O that all the world would prove
How a pard'ning God can love.
‖: How he waits for all who come ! :‖
O that all the world might see
What his grace hath done for me !
‖: How he welcomes wand'rers home. :‖

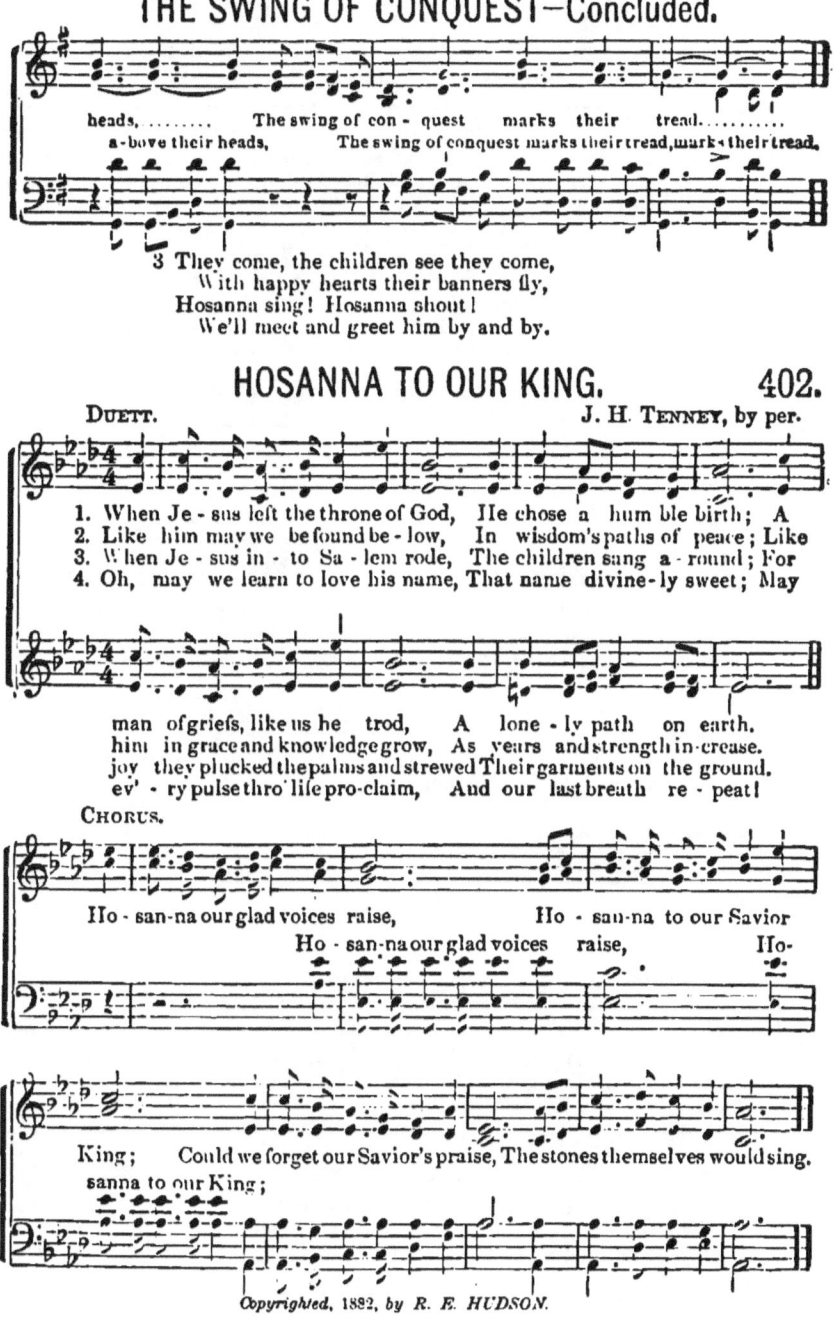

MEMORIES OE GALILEE.—Concluded.

CHORUS.

Oh, Gal-i-lee, sweet Gal-i-lee, Where Jesus lov'd so much to be, Oh,
Gal-i-lee, blue Gal-i-lee, Come sing thy song a-gain to me.

PURER IN HEART. 404.

Mrs A. L. Davison.   J. H. Fillmore. by per.

1. Pur-er in heart, O God, Help me to be; May I devote my life Whol-ly to thee. Watch thou my wayward feet,
Guide me with counsel sweet, Pur-er in heart, Help me to be.

2. Pur-er in heart, O God, Help me to be; Teach me to
do thy will Most lov-ing-ly, Be thou my friend and guide,
Let me with thee a-bide, Pur-er in heart, Help me to be.

3. Pur-er in heart, O God, Help me to be; That I thy
ho-ly face One day may see. Keep me from se-cret sin,
Reign thou my soul within, Pur-er in heart, Help me to be.

Copyrighted, 1882, by R. E. HUDSON.

WE SHALL KNOW.—Concluded.

lone, In the dawn - ing of the morning, When the
to walk alone, In the dawning of the morning,

mists have cleared a-way; In the dawn - ing of the
When the mists have cleared away, In the dawning

morn-ing, When the mists have cleared away.
When the mists have cleared away.

BLESS THE LORD. 406.

A SERVICE OF PRAISE. Words and Music by R. E. HUDSON.

1. Bless the Lord, Bless the Lord, Bless the Lord, Bless the Lord, Amen.
2. For His peace, For His peace, Bless the Lord, Bless the Lord, Amen.
3. For His love, For His love, Bless the Lord, Bless the Lord, Amen.
4. For His joy, For His joy, Bless the Lord, Bless the Lord, Amen.

Copyrighted, 1885, by R. E. HUDSON.

407. CLING CLOSER TO JESUS.

ARTHUR W. FRENCH.   *John 16:33.*   J. H. TENNEY.

1. Cling closer to Jesus, Ye weary ones, cling. And rest 'neath the shadow
2. Cling closer to Jesus, Ye penitents, cling, His mercy shall sweeten
3. Cling closer to Jesus, Come, Christian, and cling; Un-to him your troubles'

Of his mighty wing; Nor from that blest shelter Go ev-er as-tray;
The bitterest sting; His patience, his kindness Come feel while you may;
And suffering bring; He'll bear every bur-den, And lighten your way;

CHORUS.

Cling closer to Je-sus, Cling closer to-day!
Cling closer to Je-sus, Cling closer to-day! } Oh! cling to the Saviour,
Cling closer to Je-sus, Cling closer to-day!

Rit.

Your refuge and stay! Cling closer to Je-sus, Still clos-er to-day!

408. I LEFT IT ALL WITH JESUS.

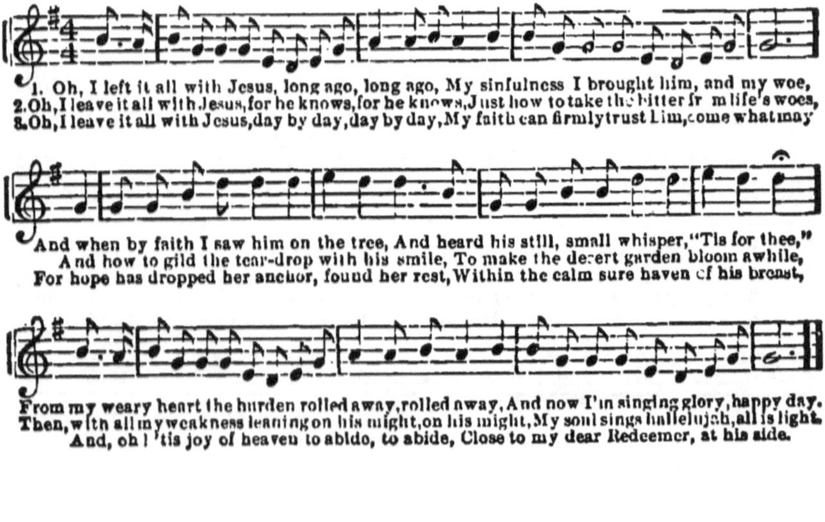

1. Oh, I left it all with Jesus, long ago, long ago, My sinfulness I brought him, and my woe,
2. Oh, I leave it all with Jesus, for he knows, for he knows, Just how to take the bitter fr m life's woes,
3. Oh, I leave it all with Jesus, day by day, day by day, My faith can firmly trust him, come what may

And when by faith I saw him on the tree, And heard his still, small whisper, "Tis for thee,"
And how to gild the tear-drop with his smile, To make the desert garden bloom awhile,
For hope has dropped her anchor, found her rest, Within the calm sure haven of his breast,

From my weary heart the burden rolled away, rolled away, And now I'm singing glory, happy day.
Then, with all my weakness leaning on his might, on his might, My soul sings hallelujah, all is light.
And, oh! 'tis joy of heaven to abide, to abide, Close to my dear Redeemer, at his side.

409. REPENT AND BELIEVE.

Fannie J. Crosby. — G. P. Benjamin, by per.

1 Stay not till to-morrow, oh, sinner, arise, To seek thy salvation, Be active, be wise; The Father is waiting his child to receive, He longs to embrace thee, repent and believe.

2 Stay not till to-morrow, this moment, improve, The Savior invites thee Reject not his love; The Savior, who languished thy soul to retrieve, This only he asks thee, repent and believe.

CHORUS.—Repent and believe, repent and believe, Oh, would'st thou be happy, repent and believe.

3 Stay not till to morrow, its light may behold,
Thy form and thy features all lifeless and cold;
The Spirit entreating, oh, why wilt thou grieve?
Be warned of thy danger, repent and believe.

4 Come, kneel at the cross where the Savior has died,
Come wash in the fountain that flows from his side;
Now trust him by faith, and a blessing receive,
He only can save thee, repent and believe.

Copyrighted, 1882, by R. E. HUDSON.

410.

1 O for a glance of heavenly day,
To take this stubborn heart away;
And thaw, with beams of love divine,
This heart, this frozen heart of mine.

2 The rocks can rend; the earth can quake
The seas can roar; the mountains shake:
Of feeling, all things show some sign,
But this unfeeling heart of mine.

3 To hear the sorrows thou hast felt,
O Lord, an adamant would melt:
But I can read each moving line,
And nothing moves this heart of mine.

4 But power divine can do the deed;
And, Lord, that power I greatly need:
Thy Spirit can from dross refine,
And melt and change this heart of mine.

2 My sins are washed away
  In the blood of the Lamb.
3 I've washed my garments white
  In the blood of the Lamb.

4 The martyrs overcame
  By the blood of the Lamb.
5 I soon shall mount the skies
  Through the blood of the Lamb.

SINKING OUT OF SELF. 413

Rev W F. Crafts.   From "WELCOME TIDINGS", by per   R. Lowry.

1. Now cru-ci-fied with Christ I am, The self with-in is slain; But still I live, and yet not I— Christ lives in me a-gain.
2. Dead to the world with sin I am, A-live to God a-lone; The life I have, I live by faith In God's be-lov-ed Son.
3. The throne of self with-in my heart The King of saints does fill; My spir-it crowns Him Lord of all, And waits to do His will.
4. Here-af-ter, "it is no more I," Nor "sin" that rul-eth me; Reign, reign for-ev-er, bles-sed Christ, My all I give to Thee.

CHORUS.
I am sinking out of self, out of self, in-to Christ, Sinking out of self in-to Christ, I am sinking sinking, sinking out of self, Sinking out of self in-to Christ.

Copyright 1875, by BIGLOW & MAIN.

414

1 I love thy church, O God!
  Her walls before thee stand,
  Dear as the apple of thine eye,
  And graven on thy hand.

2 For her my tears shall fall;
  For her my prayers ascend;
  To her my cares and toils be given,
  Till toils and cares shall end.

3 Beyond my highest joy
  I prize her heavenly ways;
  Her sweet communion, solemn vows,
  Her hymns of love and praise.

4 Sure as thy truth shall last,
  To Zion shall be given
  The brightest glories earth can yield,
  And brighter bliss of heaven.

415. STILL THERE IS ROOM.

Mrs. VANALSTYNE. S. J. VAIL, by per.

1. Thank God for the feast of the gos-pel, Where all are in-vit-ed to come;
Tho' millions have tast-ed its full-ness, O praise Him that still there is room:

CHORUS.
Still there is room, Still there is room, O praise Him that still there is room;
Still there is room, still there is room; O praise Him that still there is room, is room.

2 Come, ye that are hungry and thirsty,
　The feast is provided for you;
O come without money and purchase
　The bread that your souls will renew.

3 The pleasures of earth are but fleeting,
　Like blossoms they soon will decay;
O come to the feast of the gospel,
　Thro' Jesus, the Life and the Way.

416.

1 Behold a stranger at the door!
　He gently knocks, has knocked before,
　Has waited long, is waiting still;
　You treat no other friend so ill.
CHORUS.
　Oh, let the dear Savior come in,
　He'll cleanse the heart from sin!
　Oh, keep him no more out at the door,
　But let the dear Savior come in.

2 Oh, lovely attitude!—he stands
　With melting heart, and loaded hands,
　Oh, matchless kindness!—and he shows
　This matchless kindness to his foes!

3 But will he prove a friend indeed?
　He will—the very friend you need;
　The friend of sinners—yes, 'tis he,
　With garments dyed on Calvary.

Copyrighted, 1882, by R. E. HUDSON.

NO COMPROMISE WITH WRONG. 417.

Mrs. M. A. Collins. From "TIDAL WAVES." W. H. Doane.

With vigor.

1. Lo! a mighty host is rising now, See! their banner is unfurled!
2. See the mighty host advancing now! Look! the proud oppressors flee!
3. Weary watchers, cease your vigils now, For the morning surely comes;
4. Sing, O Zion! no more desolate, Lift thine eyes, the brightness see!

Its fair legend. Truth and Righteousness; Spread the tidings thro' the world.
So our country breaks its fetters off, And her captive sons are free.
Night is fleeing, joy is dawning now On your hearts and on your homes.
Thy Redeemer makes thee glorious, Thine oppressors bend to thee.

CHORUS.

No compromise! no compromise! No more yielding to the foe; No compromise! no compromise! No, no, no, no, no, no, NO!

418.

1 Stand up!—stand up for Jesus!
 Ye soldiers of the cross;
 Lift high his royal banner,
 It must not suffer loss;
 From victory unto victory
 His army shall be led,
 Till every foe is vanquished,
 And Christ is Lord indeed.

2 Stand up!—stand up for Jesus
 Stand in his strength alone:
 The arm of flesh will fail you—
 Ye dare not trust your own:
 Put on the gospel armor,
 And, watching unto prayer,
 Where duty calls or danger,
 Be never wanting there.

Copyright 1874, by W. H. DOANE.

421.

2
1 Only waiting till the shadows
  Are a little longer grown,
  Only waiting till the glimmer
  Of the day's last beam is flown.
Till the night of earth is faded
  From the heart once full of day,
Till the stars of heaven are breaking
  Thro' the twilight, soft and gray.

2 Only waiting till the reapers
  Have the last sheaf gathered home,
  For the Summer-time is faded,
    And the Autumn winds have come.

Quickly, reapers, quickly gather
  The last ripe hours of my heart;
For the bloom of life is withered,
  And I hasten to depart.

3 Only waiting till the angels
  Open wide the mystic gate,
At whose feet I long have lingered,
  Weary, poor, and desolate.
Even now I hear their footsteps,
  And their voices far away;
If they call me, I am waiting,
  Only waiting to obey.

422.

CLOSER TO THEE.—Concluded.

closer, still closer to Thee, Draw me, dear Saviour, still closer to Thee, to Thee.

Copyrighted, 1886, by R. E. Hudson.

A LITTLE TALK WITH JESUS. 424.

Words and Music by R. E. Hudson.

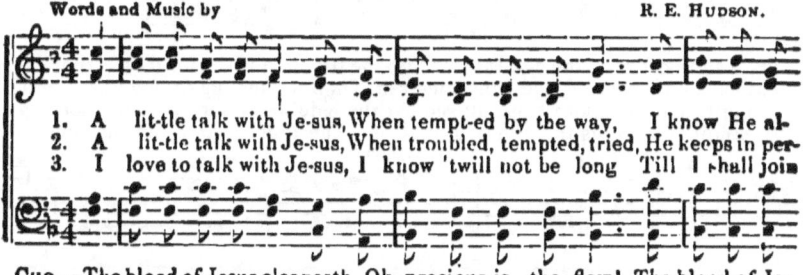

1. A lit-tle talk with Je-sus, When tempt-ed by the way, I know He al-
2. A lit-tle talk with Je-sus, When troubled, tempted, tried, He keeps in per-
3. I love to talk with Je-sus, I know 'twill not be long Till I shall join

Cho.—The blood of Jesus cleanseth, Oh, precious is the flow! The blood of Je-

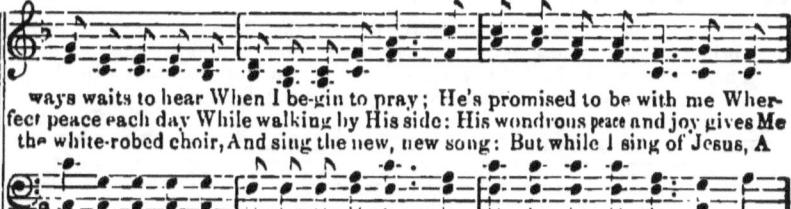

ways waits to hear When I be-gin to pray; He's promised to be with me Wher-
fect peace each day While walking by His side: His wondrous peace and joy gives Me
the white-robed choir, And sing the new, new song: But while I sing of Jesus, A

sus cleanseth now, It cleanseth white as snow; Oh, happy, happy day, when He

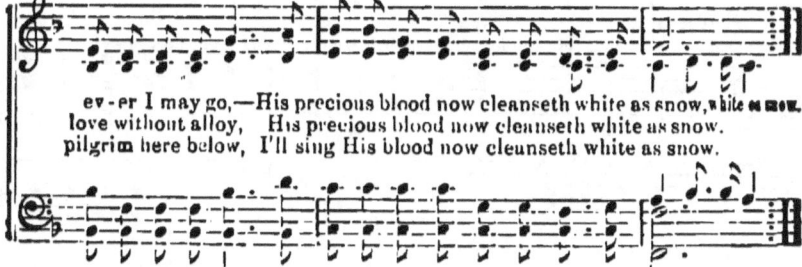

ev-er I may go,—His precious blood now cleanseth white as snow, white as snow.
love without alloy, His precious blood now cleanseth white as snow.
pilgrim here below, I'll sing His blood now cleanseth white as snow.

washed my sins away.—The blood of Jesus cleanseth white as snow.

Copyrighted, 1887, by R. E. Hudson.

WHAT A GATHERING, &c.—Concluded.

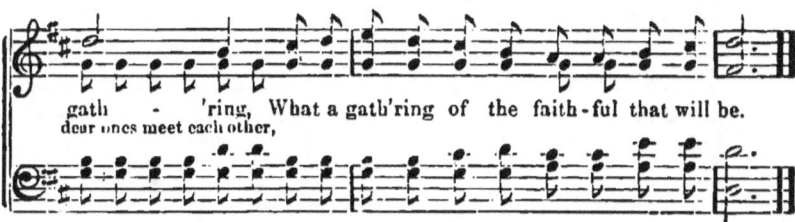

gath - 'ring, What a gath'ring of the faith-ful that will be.
dear ones meet each other,

JESUS COMES. 426.

Mrs. Phoebe Palmer.   W. J. Kirkpatrick, by per.

1. Watch, ye saints, with eyelids waking, Lo! the pow'rs of heav'n are shaking,
2. Lo! the promise of your Saviour, Pardoned sin and purchased favor,
3. Kingdoms at their base are crumbling, Hark! his chariot wheels are rumbling,
4. Nations wane, though proud and stately, Christ his kingdom hasteneth greatly,

Keep your lamps all trimmed and burning, Ready for your Lord's returning.
Blood-washed robes and crowns of glory: Haste to tell Redemption's story.
Tell, oh, tell of grace abounding, While the seventh trump is sounding.
Earth her latest pangs is summing, Shout, ye saints, your Lord is coming.

Refrain. Lo! he comes, he comes all glorious, Jesus comes to reign victorious.

Repeat Refrain.

Lo! he comes, Lo! Je - sus comes.
Lo! he comes,   (*Omit.*)   Yes, Je - sus comes.

5 Lamb of God! thou meek and lowly,
Judah's Lion! high and holy, [thee,"
Lo! thy "Bride comes forth to meet
All in blood-washed robes to greet thee.

6 Sinners come, while Christ is pleading,
Now for you he's interceding;
Haste, ere grace and time diminished,
Shall proclaim the mystery finished.

427. THE HIDING-PLACE IS NIGH.

Isaac Watts. — *R. E. Hudson.*

1. Salvation! Oh, the joyful sound! What pleasure to our ears!
 A sovereign balm for every wound, A cordial for our fears.
2. Salvation! let the echo fly The spacious earth around,
 While all the armies of the sky Conspire to raise the sound.
3. Salvation! Oh, thou bleeding Lamb, To thee the praise belongs!
 Salvation shall inspire our hearts, And dwell upon our tongues.

CHORUS.
He is the only refuge—fly! There's danger in delay.
Sinners, the hiding-place is nigh; The Saviour calls—away!

---

428. TUNE—ZION. D.

1 Zion stands with hills surrounded,
  Zion, kept by power divine.
 All her foes shall be confounded,
  Though the world in arms combine;
   Happy Zion—
 What a favored lot is thine!

2 Every human tie may perish;
  Friend to friend unfaithful prove;
 Mothers cease their own to cherish;
  Heaven and earth at last remove;
   But no changes
 Can attend Jehovah's love.

3 In the furnace God may prove thee,
  Thence to bring thee forth more bright;
 But can never cease to love thee;
  Thou art precious in his sight;
   God is with thee—
 God, thine everlasting light.

429. TUNE—ZION. D.

1 Guide me, O Thou great Jehovah,
  Pilgrim through this barren land:
 I am weak, but Thou art mighty;
  Hold me with Thy powerful hand:
   Bread of heaven,
 Feed me till I want no more.

2 Open now the crystal fountain,
  Whence the healing waters flow;
 Let the fiery, cloudy pillar
  Lead me all my journey through:
   Strong Deliverer,
 Be Thou still my strength and shield.

3 When I tread the verge of Jordan,
  Bid my anxious fears subside;
 Bear me through the swelling current,
  Lead me safe on Canaan's side;
   Songs of praises
 I will ever give to Thee.

3 My mistakes his free grace will cover,
My sins he will wash away,
And the feet that shrink and falter
Shall walk thro' the gates of day.

4 The mistakes of my life have been many,
And my spirit is sick with sin,
And I scarce can see for weeping,
But the Savior will let me in.

Copyrighted, 1882, by R. E. HUDSON.

435. THE GRACE OF GOD.

"My grace is sufficient for thee; for my strength is made perfect in weakness."

Viola.   J. G. DAILEY.

1. Thy grace, O my Saviour, has wrought us release, When sin and temptation were
2. We know we are weak, and we're thoughtless at times, We murmur and grieve Thee, our
3. O send us Thy Spirit, Lord, keep us from sin, And lend us in pathways of

[its stead

nigh; And weakness soon vanished when Thee we besought, Thy strength in
Friend; But Father, we love Thee! Thou knowest we do, Yet loving, how can
peace; Our Father, O graciously grant us thy strength, 'Twill always afford

CHORUS.

to sup-ply.   In my weakness   I am strengthened
we of-fend!
us re-lease.   I am strengthened   In my weakness,

In my weakness   I am strengthened,   In my weakness
       I am strengthened   In my weakness,

Repeat pp.

       I am strengthened,   Made stronger by the grace of God.
I am strengthened   In my weakness,

DON'T BE TOO LATE.—Concluded.

Copyrighted, by R. E. Hudson, 1884.

HE IS MINE. 441

Words and Music by E. A. Hoffman.

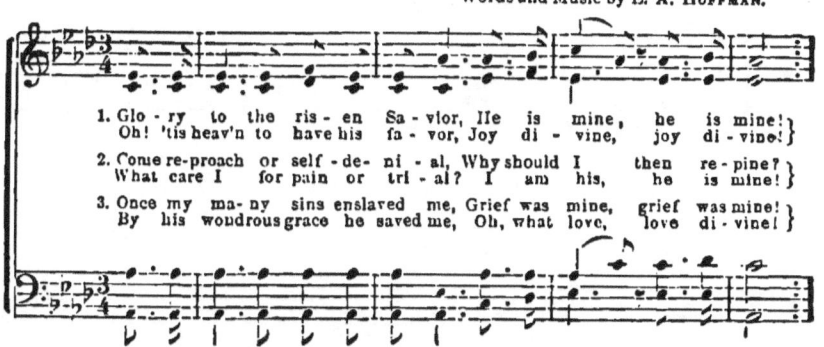

1. Glo-ry to the ris-en Sa-vior, He is mine, he is mine!
   Oh! 'tis heav'n to have his fa-vor, Joy di-vine, joy di-vine!
2. Come re-proach or self-de-ni-al, Why should I then re-pine?
   What care I for pain or tri-al? I am his, he is mine!
3. Once my ma-ny sins enslaved me, Grief was mine, grief was mine!
   By his wondrous grace he saved me, Oh, what love, love di-vine!

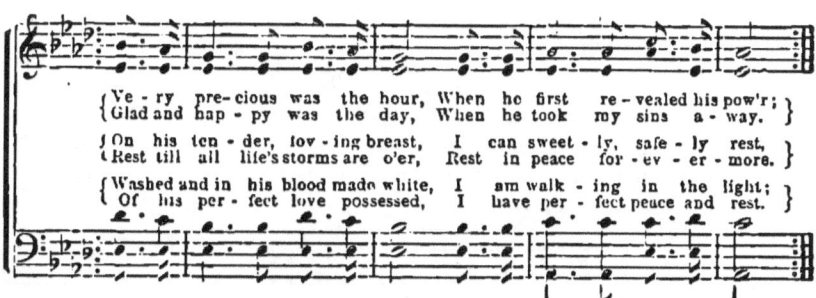

Ve-ry pre-cious was the hour, When he first re-vealed his pow'r;
Glad and hap-py was the day, When he took my sins a-way.
On his ten-der, lov-ing breast, I can sweet-ly, safe-ly rest,
Rest till all life's storms are o'er, Rest in peace for-ev-er-more.
Washed and in his blood made white, I am walk-ing in the light;
Of his per-fect love possessed, I have per-fect peace and rest.

Refrain.

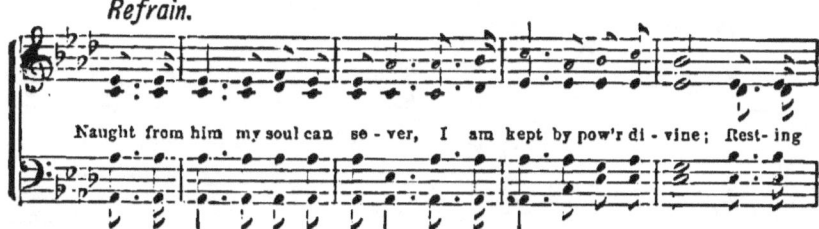

Naught from him my soul can se-ver, I am kept by pow'r di-vine; Rest-ing

in his love for-ev-er, I am his,...... he is mine!

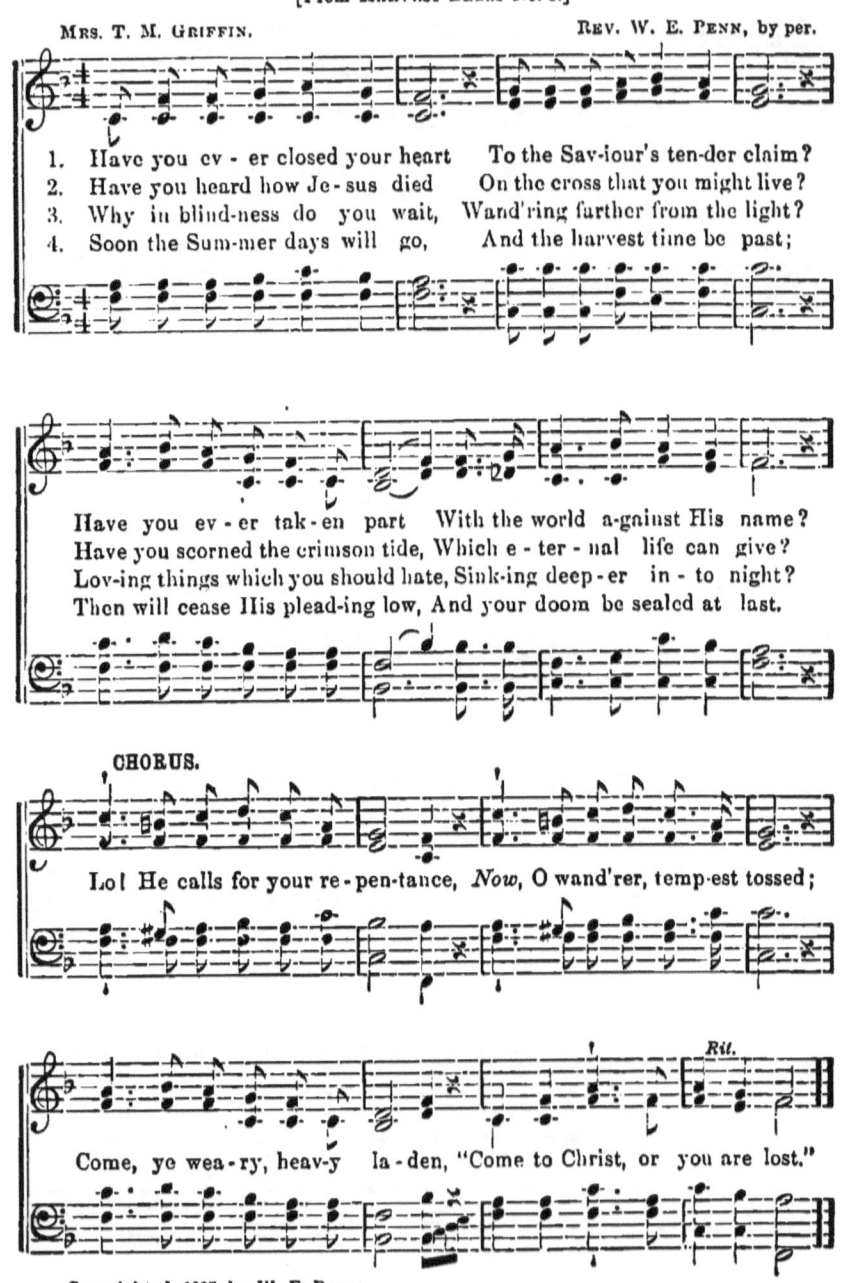

BENEVENTO. G

How tedious and tasteless the hours,
  When Jesus no longer I see;
Sweet prospects, sweet birds and sweet flowers,
  Have all lost their sweetness to me;
The midsummer sun shines but dim,
  The fields strive in vain to look gay
But when I am happy in him,
  December's as pleasant as May.

His Name yields the richest perfume,
  And sweeter than music his voice;
His presence disperses my gloom,
  And makes all within me rejoice;
I should, were he always thus nigh,
  Have nothing to wish or to fear;
No mortal so happy as I,—
  My summer would last all the year.

Content with beholding His face,
  My all to His pleasure resigned,
No changes of season or place
  Would make any change in my mind
While blest with a sense of his love,
  A palace a toy would appear;
And prisons would palaces prove,
  If Jesus would dwell with me there.

OLD, OLD STORY. G

I love to tell the story
  Of Unseen things above,
Of Jesus and His glory,
  Of Jesus and his love;
I love to tell the story,
  Because I know its true
It satisfies my longings,
  As nothing else would do.
Cho.—I love to tell the story,
  'Twill be my theme in glory,
To tell the old, old story,
  Of Jesus and his love.

I love to tell the story;
  More wonderful it seems
Than all the golden fancies
  Of all the golden dreams,
I love to tell the story;
  It did so much for me!
And that is just the reason
  I tell it now to thee.

I love to tell the story
  For those who know it best,
Seem hungering and thirsting
  To hear it like the rest.
And when in Scenes of glory,
  I sing the new, new song,
'Twill be the old, old story,
  That I have loved so long.

NINTY AND NINE. A

There were ninety and nine
  that safely lay
In the shelter of the fold,
But one was out on the hills away,
Far off from the gates of gold—
Away on the mountains wild and bare
Away from the tender shepherds care‖

"Lord thou hast here
  Thy ninety and nine:
Are they not enough for Thee?"
But the shepherd made answer: this of mine
Has wandered away from me;
‖And although the road be rough and steep,
I go to the desert to find my sheep‖

But none of the ransomed ever knew
  How deep were the waters crossed,
Nor how dark was the night
  That the Lord passed through
Ere he found His sheep that was lost.
  ‖Out in the desert he heard its cry-
Sick and helpless, and ready to die.‖

MUSIC No. 157.

With panting heart that dares to seek
The fullness of Thy love Divine,
I lay me at Thy bleeding feet,
And claim Thy promises as mine.

  Cho.—I believe, I believe,
    The priceless gifts I now receive:
  Thy blood doth cleanse,
    And make me whole,
  Thy perfect love fill all my soul,
    I believe, I believe,
  The priceless gift I now receive.

My groans and tears
No change have wrought
They fail my nature to refine,
The power and love
Thy groans have bought,
By simple faith henceforth are **mine**.

Oh, let my heart forever be
The home in which
Thou lov'st to dwell;
Renewed and filled with love to Thee
Endued with power that love to tell.

MORE THAN I ASKED OR THOUGHT. 446

FRANCES RIDLEY HAVERGAL. 1 Cor. 2:9. J. B. FERGUSON.

1. How shall I praise thee, Saviour dear, For this new life so sweet, For taking the poor gift I laid At thy beloved feet, Keeping thy hand upon my heart, To still each anxious beat!

2. Oh! thou hast done far more for me Than I had asked or thought! I stand and marvel to behold What thou, my Lord, hast wrought, And wonder what glad lessons yet I shall be daily taught!

How shall I praise thee, Saviour dear, For this new life so sweet!
Oh! thou hast done far more for me Than I had asked or thought!

3. I never thought it could be thus—
Month after month to know
The river of thy peace without
One ripple in its flow,
Without one quiver in the trust,
One flicker in its glow.
I never thought it could be thus—
That I such peace should know.

4. Dear Lord! I find thy promise true,
Of perfect peace and rest;
I cannot sigh—I can but sing
While leaning on thy breast,
And leaving everything to thee
Whose ways are always best.
Oh! matchless is the sovereign grace
That brings such peace and rest!

447. VICTORY.

Harmonized and arranged R. E. H.
Rev. W. O. Pierce.

1. O turn ye, O turn ye, for why will ye die, When God in great mer-cy is com-ing so nigh? Now Je-sus in-vites you, the Spir-it says, "Come," And an-gels are wait-ing to wel-come you home.
2. And now Christ is read-y your souls to receive, O how can you question, if you will be-lieve? If sin is your bur-den, why will you not come? 'Tis you he bids wel-come; he bids you come home.
3. Why will you be starving, and feed-ing on air? There's mer-cy in Je-sus, e-nough and to spare; If still you are doubting, make tri-al and see, And prove that his mer-cy is boundless and free.

CHORUS.

Oh come, come to Je-sus, oh come to-day; The Spir-it in-vites you now, oh come without de-lay, A home and a mansion is prepared for thee, Halle-lu-jah to Je-sus, for the vic-to-ry.

Copyrighted, 1882, by R. E. HUDSON.

PARDONED. 451
Matt. 9:2. J. H. Tenney.

1. Sorrowing sinner, weep no more; Christ is stand-ing at the door;
Haste, and on his pierc-ed feet Pour thy heart's ob-la-tion sweet;
He will love thee, He will love thee, And will leave thee nev-ermore.

2. He hath seen the bended knee;
He hath heard thy contrite plea;
Not in vain thy soul hath wept;
Not in vain its vigil kept.
While yet praying, hear him saying:
"All thy sins I bear for thee."

3. Saved from wrath and sanctified
Thro' the blood of his dear side,
Never from thy happy heart
Let the heavenly guest depart;
He is with thee; Bid him with thee
Ever, evermore abide.

HIS PROMISE I RECEIVE. 452
John 3:16. R. E. Hudson.

1. Come, O my God, the promise seal, This mountain, sin, remove.
2. Let an-ger, sloth, desire and pride, This moment be subdued;

Now in my wait-ing soul re-veal The vir-tue of thy love.
Be cast in-to the crimson tide Of my Redeemer's blood.

D.S. come to him, I trust in him, I will—I do be-lieve.

CHORUS.
By faith, by faith in Je-sus' blood, His promise I re-ceive; I

3. Saviour, to thee my soul looks up,
My present Saviour thou!
In all the confidence of hope
I claim the blessing now.

4. 'Tis done: thou dost this moment save,
With full salvation bless;
Redemption through thy blood I have,
And spotless love and peace.

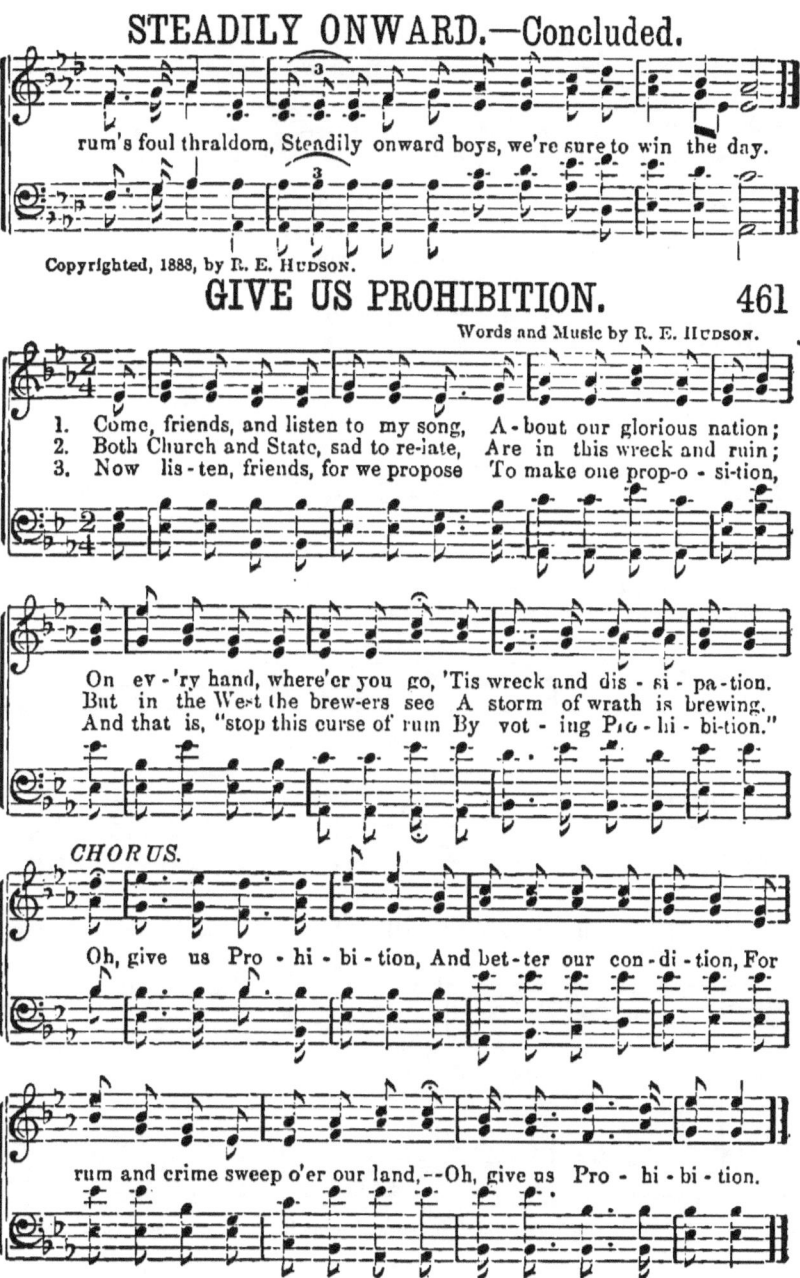

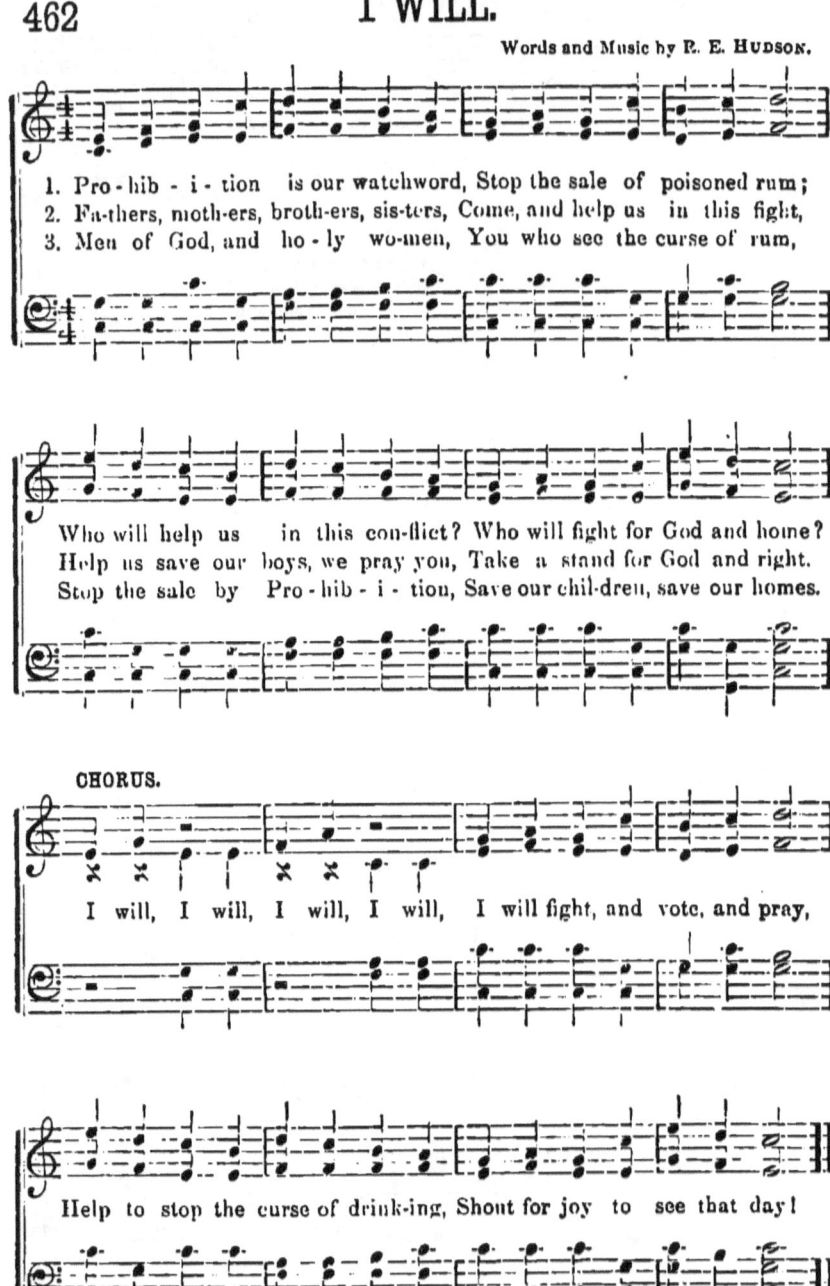

INDEX.

At the cross	81	Come unto me	17—365
Angels are looking	89	Come to Christ	50
Alone with Jesus	93	Cast thy bread	53
Awake my soul	111	Church Rallying song	78
And can I yet delay	112	Christ is all	90
A charge to keep I have	119	Coming home to-night	92
At the fountain	355	Cold water for me	107
A thousand years	152	Come ye sinners	110
All hail the power	170	Come to me	135
Asleep in Jesus	188	Consecration	150—161
A Sinner like me	194	Coronation	163
Autumn	217	Close to thee	174
America	226	Come oh my soul	203
Antioch	235	Cleansing Wave	201
Arise my soul	240	Communion	210
Avon	243	Come every soul by sin	212
Altered motto	266	Come Holy Spirit	222
All in all	328	Come let us join	239
Able to save	370	Come to him now	254
At the cross I'll abide	377	Child of the King	290
All the way it is Jesus	400	Clinging to the cross	301
A little talk with Jesus	424	Church of God awake	308
A child of the King of kings	52	Calvary	314
Alas and did my Savior	156	Cleansing Balm	316
Anticipation	276	Come and help us	335
		Come ye that love	146
Beautiful beckoning hands	15	Coming home again	385
Behold the Bridegroom	43	Cling closer to Jesus	407
Beautiful city of gold	54	Closer to thee	423
Blessed name	67	Children of the heavenly King	77
Be guiding me	103	Companionship with Jesus	395
Beulah land	199		
Blest be the tie that binds	247	Daughter of Zion	143
Better wish	291	Death is coming	22
Blessed assurance	292	Daily Victory	87
Bringing in the sheaves	293	Duane street	160
Blessd Jesus	336	Deliverance will come	186
Bless the Lord	406	Dennis	244
Behold a Stranger	416	Duke street	245
Blow ye the trumpet	241	Desert	255
Beautiful hands	281	Disturb not my dreaming	287
Bethany	122	Delay not to come	392
Balm in Gilead	154		

Enough for me	355	How firm a foundation	350
Exhortation	390	Have you been to Jesus	357
		Homeward bound	381
For you and for me	82	Hear Jesus knocking	389
Fill me now	95	Hear him calling	285
Full salvation	298	Hosanna to our king	402
Falling leaves	421	He came to save me	35
Free at last	56		
Fade, fade each earthly joy	121	I'v washed my robes	6
Follow thou me	144	I come just as I am	23
Father I stretch my hands	145	I hope to meet you all	24
Forever here my rest shall be	352–145	I'm satisfied	32
Fathers house	8	I love thy church	414
		I'm believing	41
God be with you	7	If you want pardon	60
Go preach	14	I leave it all with Jesus	408
Gospel feast	20	I am saved	65
Glory, honor to his name	62	I have taken up the cross	70
Gathering home	101	I will God helping me	72
Glory to his name	117	I shall never know a sorrow	88
Gloria	124	I'll live for him	105
Gather at the river	137	I need thee every hour	118
Great Physician	168	I love to tell the story	126
Glory to the Lamb	177–412	Is your lamp burning	399
Going home	184	I'm so glad	131
Guide	228	I'll be there	136
God is coming	288	I am Jesus' little lamb	348
Glorious fountain	342	I would not live alway	149
Gates of the beautiful	379	I am coming to the cross	173
Gospel train	394	I am coming Lord	181
Guide me O thou	429	I'm going home	187
		I saw a happy pilgrim	190
		I will sing you a song	191
His Yoke is easy	3	I love to think of that	196
Happy on the way	13	I was once far away	198
He comes o'er my soul	25	I do believe	200
Homeward bound	40	In evil long I took delight	213
Happy tidings	42	I've been redeemed	230
Handwriting on the wall	44	I am far frae my hame	282
He rolled the stone away	48	In the shadow of his wings	289
He is calling	59	I will give you rest	322
His name is Jesus	66	I am the light	388
He is coming	74	Is not this the land	331
Half has never been told	79	I will guide thee	353
How tedious and tasteless	125	I will follow	358
He leadeth me	346	I rest upon his promise	366
He dies the friend, sinners	164	Increase our faith	376
Heavenly Shore	193		
Hail thou once despised Jesus	220	Jesus is strong to deliver	27
Hark the voice	221	Joy among the angels	31
Holy Spirit	231	Jesus thine all viciorious love	72
How sweet the name of	232	Jesus is calling	109
He ransomed me	259	Jesus my all	120
Hail Him King	270	Jesus I my cross have taken	132
He will gather the wheat	299	Jesus saves me all the time	347
Have you the garment	304	Jesus lover of my soul	161–320
He would not go away	311	Just as I am without one	223
He knows	349	Joy to the world	238

Title	No.
Jesus the name that charms	208
Just waiting	319
Jesus only	330
Jesus is ready	363
Jesus now is passing	367
Jesus will give you rest	368
Jesus comes to save	373
Jesus lead the way	419
Just the same to-day	96
Let me hide in thy wounds	19
Let him in	39
Lead me to the rock	38
Life for a look	75
Living waters flow	76
Lead me gently home	83
Lead me safely on	86
Look to Jesus	106
Lord I am thine	224
Love divine all love	225
Lenox	236
Love of Christ	274
Looking unto Jesus	294
Lilly of the valley	306
Life of trust	339
Life boat	372
Love offering	383
Lost and found	397
Lo, he comes	426
Let us sing of His love	189
Meet me there	46
Meditation	55
Marching on	61
Mighty march	64
Mighty to keep	130
My sins are under the blood	133
Mear	156
Martyn	158
My body soul and spirit	172
My days are gliding	179
My Savior suffered on the cross	180
My faith looks up to thee	229
My soul be on thy guard	248
My spirit is free	258
My angel mother	283
Mary Magdalan	307
My Savior knows	359
My offering	378
Memories of Gallilee	403
My dream	155
My name written there	183
My Jesus I love thee	140
My hope is built	147
Nearer my God to thee	122
Ninety and nine	127
Neath his wing	318
No room in heaven	396
No compromise	417
Only Jesus	18
Oh, 'twas love	28
Old yet ever new	49
Only near to the kingdom	80
O, to be nothing	100
Over there	114
O happy day	157
Of him who did it	163
O how happy are they	197
Ortinville	227
O for a faith	233
O for a closer walk	234
Oh that my load of sin	251
Only thee	262
Our cherished loved one	279
O worship the Lord	360
Old mountain pines	371
O for a thousand tongues	391
Oh for a glance of	410
Oh 'tis glory	411
Only waiting	422
O now I see the	204
O for a heart to praise	390
O thou in whose presence	55
Press the battle on	5
Praise God from	243
Prodigal child come home	273
Prayer for guidance	284
Peace divine	312
Peace at last	327
Perfect peace	142
Peace be still	362
Precious spirit	369
Purer in heart	404
Rejoicing evermore	21
Roll the stone away	45
Resting by and by	84
Room at the cross	99
Rockingham	237
Rock of Ages	249
Resting	257
Rewarded	275
Redeeming love	278
Redeemed	315
Rose of Sharon	326
Ring the bells	343
Repent and believe	409
Sitting at the feet of Jesus	33
Sing oh sing	141
Saved by grace alone	73
Say, are you ready	85
Signal lights	94
Some sweet day	104

Suffer the children to come	123
Sunshine in the soul	129
Safely hide me	134
Sweet by and by	138
Sweeping through the gates	151
Sleeper in Zion, awake	153
Savior breathe an evening	206
Silently the shades are falling	207
Show pity, Lord	250
Sing of his love	264
Sowing and reaping	267
Stand the storm	270
Since I have been	271
Sweetly resting	295
Seek ye the Kingdom of God	296
Sing of my redeemer	300
Stay sinner, stay	317
Sailing on the sea	324
Safety	325
Satisfied	337
Simply trusting	340
Swing of conquest	401
Sinking out of self	413
Still there is room	415
Stand up, stand up for	418
Silent night	420
Salvation, oh the joyful saved	427
Saved to the uttermost	303
Soldiers of Christ arise	5
Take my heart dear Jesus	9
The waters of Jordan	11
Treasures of heaven	30
The unseen city	36
Take all my sins away	47
They come	57
The road to heaven	69
The Lord is my light	71
The ten virgins	91
Trust all to Jesus	98
The open fountain	102
The light of truth is breaking	108
Take my hand	113
This love so free	345
Tell it to Jesus	375
The morning light is	162
The great Physician now is here	171
Take me as I am	175
'Twas rum	253
The Savior stands waiting	261
The harvest is passing	260
The cross is all my glory	297
There's cleansing in the blood	305
There'll be joy in the morning	321
The shadow of the rock	323
Touch it not	329
To-morrow it may be too late	333
Trust a little longer	334
Trusting in the promise	361
The new song	364–398
The golden light	374
The shining ones of	380
This is why I love my	384
The throne in my heart	393
The burden bearer came	34
Thy will be done	334
Up for Jesus stand	268
Vain delusive world	182
Weighed in the balance	309
Who shall be able	310
Welcome to glory	313
We will pray for one	332
Wonderful fountain	338
Won't we have a happy time	341
Work for the night is coming	148
Why don't you come to Jesus	356
What shall it profit	382
White as snow	386
Work and wait	387
We Shall know	405
What a gathering that will be	425
Wonderful Love	2
When the glad day comes	4
Wash me in the blood	10
Wondrous love	12
Whiter than snow	16 165
Weary one rest	26
What did Jesus say	29
We conquer	51
Who's on the Lords side	58
We shall sing	63
We shall stand before the	68
We are walking in the	77
Wonderful Savior	97
Waiting	115
What a friend we have in Jesus	116
With panting heart	128
We'll work	139
Webb	159
We praise Thee, oh God	214
When I can read	205
While life prolongs its	242
When all thy mercies	246
Who'll enlist	252
When we arrive at home	256
Wandering stranger	265
Will you be washed	272
When he makes up his	277
Will you stand	302
We shall meet Him	215
Yield not to temptations	216
Zion stands with hills	428

www.ingramcontent.com/pod-product-compliance
Lightning Source LLC
Chambersburg PA
CBHW020246240426
43672CB00006B/658